Praise for *The Post-Church Christian*

Eavesdropping may not always be polite, but listening in on this conversation is something you won't want to miss, especially if you want to understand the delicate dynamics of the generation gap between boomers and millennials. With clarity and transparency, Paul Nyquist and his son Carson navigate the whitewater of generational disconnect and provide for us a valuable seminar on understanding and reconnecting with those whose worldviews are dramatically different. Highly recommended!

> —JOE STOWELL
> President, Cornerstone University

The Nyquists, father and son, represent respectively the boomers and the millennials and they communicate very well with each other on matters of faith in general and the modern church in particular. Not surprisingly, they have differences which they air with grace and conviction, but they go far beyond that as they seek mutual understanding and practical ways of bridging the gaps between them. The result is a timely book, honest, insightful written from a deep desire to be genuinely helpful.

> —Stuart Briscoe
> Author, international speaker, and too old to be
> either boomer or millennial

This book avoids simplistic responses, over-generalizations, and the blame game. Respect, integrity, and vulnerability characterize each page. I encourage ministry leaders of my generation to read this book, to take the issues raised seriously, and to continue the conversation with millennials in your ministry. I encourage millennials to read this book, to look for mentors among the boomer generation, and to join together with them for the sake of the gospel. The needs are great and the challenges severe but the resources in the church are sufficient for the task.

—GLENN R. KREIDER
Professor of Theological Studies,
Dallas Theological Seminary

This is rare. Two different generations of Christians speaking with candor, care and passion on how to do church, live on mission, and love God. Paul and Carson have given us a gift— a picture of how the church might live united in love across the generational spectrum. Church leaders, small groups and pastors would do well to buy this book in bulk and to read it together!

—BRYAN HALFERTY
College/Young Adult Pastor,
Editor of theunitive.com

This book is more than content! It's certainly that, but it's a dynamic illustration and very helpful model of how different generations should and must communicate. Sharing, being honest, listening, processing, and being teachable are reflected from cover to cover. This is adult-to-adult communication at its best between a boomer father and his millennial son, even though it reflects the older guiding the younger.

This is biblical! Without it, generational differences within families and within the church can evolve into separation and even alienation. With it, we'll walk side by side, arm in arm—not always agreeing—but nevertheless reflecting Jesus Christ as we mature together. My good friends, Paul and Carson, show us how! So read, reflect, and respond!

—**DR. GENE A. GETZ**
President, Center for Church Renewal
Pastor Emeritus, Chase Oaks Church, Plano, TX

If the church is to reclaim a credible voice in our culture, the world's largest generations (the boomers and millennials) will have to learn to work together. Paul and Carson Nyquist, father and son, have begun a conversation I pray will continue around your dinner table, your local coffee shop, and your pulpit for years to come. May God raise up a new generation of leaders even greater than the last.

—**THOM S. RAINER**
President of LifeWay Christian Resources, author of *The Millennials* (B&H Publishing Group)

In a world that so quickly pushes one extreme or another, *The Post-Church Christian* offers a balanced perspective on the gap that exists between the boomer and millennial generations. I appreciate both the language that Carson uses to embody the perspective of the millennials, as well as the gracious yet candid response from his father, Paul. To have an "insider's view" on their conversation is extremely helpful—whether for the millennial, giving voice to the experience of their faith journey, or the boomer, understanding the serious implications of future leadership and what it takes to engage the next generation. This book is necessary for anyone serious about building a bridge between the two generations.

—**BEN STEWART**
Director of Envision: Raising Up the Next Generation for Kingdom Change

In a culture where people of faith often seem all too eager to draw battle lines, *The Post-Church Christian* exchanges the typical shouting match for a refreshingly honest, candid, fireside chat. Not one ounce of dialogue or theological viewpoint is sacrificed, yet Paul and Carson are able to navigate complicated cultural paradigm shifts while propelling readers closer TO Jesus rather than pushing them further away. It's high time we move this conversation forward, and *The Post-Church Christian* is a fantastic way to kick things off.

—**MATT CHAMBERS**
Cofounder and Director of SafeWorld

THE POST-CHURCH CHRISTIAN

dealing with the generational baggage of our faith

J. PAUL NYQUIST and CARSON NYQUIST

MOODY PUBLISHERS

CHICAGO

All Scripture quotations are taken from *The Holy Bible, English Standard Version.* Copyright © 2000, 2001 by Crossway Bibles, a division of Good News Publishers. Used by permission. All rights reserved.

Edited by Bailey Utecht
Interior design: Ragont Design
Cover design: Brock, Sharp & Associates / Faceout Studio

Library of Congress Cataloging-in-Publication Data

Nyquist, J. Paul.
 The post-church Christian : dealing with the generational baggage of our faith / J. Paul Nyquist and Carson Nyquist.
     pages cm
  Includes bibliographical references (pages   ).
  ISBN 978-0-8024-0640-8
  1. Church history—20th century. 2. Church history—21st century.
3. Generation Y—Religious life. 4. Intergenerational communication—Religious aspects—Christianity. 5. Intergenerational relations—Religious aspects—Christianity. I. Nyquist, Carson. II. Title.
BR481.N97 2013
277.3'083—dc23

                                                                    2012039693

We hope you enjoy this book from Moody Publishers. Our goal is to provide high-quality, thought-provoking books and products that connect truth to your real needs and challenges. For more information on other books and products written and produced from a biblical perspective, go to www.moodypublishers.com or write to:

Moody Publishers
820 N. LaSalle Boulevard
Chicago, IL 60610

1 3 5 7 9 10 8 6 4 2

Printed in the United States of America

Dedication

from J. Paul Nyquist

To my parents, Carroll and Rose,
you understood the difference in our generations
but never stopped loving me.

To Natalie, Taylor, Carson, and Sawyer,
the millennials God gave me,
may you always love Jesus and His bride.

◆ ◆ ◆

from Carson Nyquist

To Maggie, who taught me love is never
the result of ignorance or denial
but the reward of honesty.

Contents

Introduction
Welcoming a
Post-Church Generation

When cultures collide, there is always friction. The trick is not allowing the heat to start a fire.

This book started as a normal conversation between father and son. We were enjoying a rare day together over the holidays and were catching up on life. The conversation took a new twist when Carson revealed his mounting frustrations with the church. Not a particular church. *The* church. The evangelical church. The church tradition I (Paul) had served as a pastor and leader for three decades.

My interest raised, the talk continued. Carson was not alone. Many of his millennial friends shared similar feelings of disillusionment. Their stories resonated with each other.

Some were still in the church. Many had left. All were believers in Christ and had been raised in the evangelical church. They'd done the AWANA thing. They'd led their youth groups. They knew the routine. In short, they were not the "bad" kids.

But now, they were taking the exit door. At first it was just a few. Now many more were following in their wake. Their destination was unknown. They still loved Jesus passionately. They still wanted to serve Him with their lives. But how? And where? Confused and hurt, they began searching for alternatives. Some had ideas of where to go, while others were unsure of their options.

IT'S ABOUT YOU

You are one of the 80 million millennials born between 1982 and 2000. You shared life with your baby boomer parents and perhaps a couple siblings. You experienced the unique qualities of their parenting, including an unprecedented level of coddling. Most of you were affirmed, prodded, molded but not often criticized.

You grew up in a digital world, intuitively mastering the latest technological gadgets. You grew up in a divorce-ridden society, with many of your friends coming from single-parent or blended families. You grew up in a land overloaded with debt but unable to control spending.

You also grew up in the church. A Bible-believing church —maybe a large one with a vast array of programs and services. You came to faith in Christ there. You were baptized there. You were taught the Bible there. It was home.

But it's not home anymore. Maybe you still attend on Sundays, but your heart has been wounded. Guilt kept you from leaving earlier. But now you have at least one foot out the door. And unless something changes, you'll be gone. You still love Jesus, but you are dissatisfied with the church. You're hurt, yet looking toward a better future.

A post-church Christian.

This is your story. This book is for you.

WHY THIS BOOK?

In the past few years, considerable research has clearly documented the millennial migration from the church. David Kinnaman provided groundbreaking research in his books *unChristian* and *You Lost Me*.[1] Others have picked up the same torch and helped the church expand their understanding of your generation. While dismissing this topic is impossible, many will try to avoid the issue.[2] This is where we join the dialogue.

The conversation Carson and I had over that holiday gave birth to this book. We do not pretend to be researchers, nor will this book move those pegs forward. We applaud and affirm the careful study already done on many fronts.

This book differs from other works in three important ways. First, it is written to you, a millennial. Many have sought to describe you to the boomer generation, which is useful and necessary. The goal of those books is to help the older generation understand you and the reality of your frustrations. For those who question if this gap is real, or wonder if this gap is any different from generational conflicts in the past, these books need to be the first stop. They do well in answering those questions.

But this book is written to you and others in the millennial generation. We don't want to describe you; we want to talk with you.

Second, this book is different in that we write as representatives of both generations. Carson is thoroughly millennial. I am a clear product of the baby boomer generation. This generational conversation offers understanding and healing. As we wrote and processed, it often felt like a counseling session between generations.

Yet we go beyond mere generational differences. We also converse as father and son. This is helpful as some of your frustrations may spill past the church to your parents. Your hurt growing up may be due to a pastor; it may also be due to Mom and Dad.

We get that. We experience that. This book is not just about a millennial talking with a boomer. It is also about a son working out differences with his father.

Furthermore, we are both theologically trained and committed to the local church. I served as a pastor for nearly two decades and have a deep passion for its mission in this world. Carson graduated from seminary and now serves with a church in Wisconsin. We are not outsiders to the conversation.

A boomer and a millennial. A father and a son. Both committed to the success and future of the church.

Finally, through our conversation, we want to help you deal with your baggage. Growing up in the church has left many millennials hurt, frustrated, and disillusioned. It's time to deal with the generational baggage of your faith. Until you do, it will continue to weigh you down.

WELCOME TO THE STORY

For those outside the millennial generation or experience, we also welcome you to the conversation. But know that this book is about people. Not doctrinal truth. Not theological propositions. Not institutional policies.

For those outside of this experience, our hope is that, even if you disagree with some of what we write, you will come away with a new understanding of this problem present in many churches and perhaps a new understanding of what you can do about it. As you read, you might gain a new awareness or perspective of your own pain or frustration. In that moment, we pray you'll develop a fresh sense of grace and empathy.

For your generation. And for yourself.

AN OVERVIEW

This book is organized in three parts. Carson writes part 1. He will identify and give voice to your frustrations with the existing evangelical church. The language is emotive and direct. He knows your pain. He draws upon his experiences and the stories of others.

In part 2, I want to help you begin processing things by addressing the tough questions your generation is asking. Can I love Jesus and not love the church? Can the church change and ditch its sad reputation? What do I do with the alienation I feel? Your questions deserve clear answers. In fact, the future of the church depends upon you working through these issues. With baby boomers retiring at a rate of 10,000 per day, they will mostly pass from the leadership of the church in the next ten to fifteen years.[3]

In part 3, we shift our focus from what's happening now to what's happening next. Both Carson and I will conclude with a future perspective.

As future leaders of the church, now is the time to deal with the past.

Welcome to the conversation.

Part 1

A Millennial's Perspective on the Generational Divide

Carson Nyquist

1

First Conservative Church of . . .

We love Jesus but are unsure about the church. Despite it being a familiar place, the church has deeply hurt us. In like fashion to a family, those closest to you can be quickest to draw blood.

To us the church is often a place of frustration, anger, and disillusionment. While most of us grew up in the church, we now feel alienated because of our differences. Written off as arrogant, careless, or idealistic, we are leaving the church still holding on to the hope of following Jesus.

"REAL" CHRISTIANITY

Since we were children, our generation has been enamored with reality. The birth of reality TV only fueled this desire. We revel in knowing intimate details about our favorite characters as they compete on an island or fall in love.

The value of reality has also affected our personal lives. Few generations before us are so quick to acknowledge failure. Our vulnerability and openness to share about our lives is clear to everyone. We see this as beneficial, letting people see our true self.

Pop culture only continues our education as celebrities boldly display their lives to the world. Their breakups and hookups are covered in explicit detail. We love it. We also find their mistakes posted for all to see. Yet we are quick to welcome them back. We accept their mistakes because we know we make mistakes. We forgive because we know we need forgiveness.

Our generation is messed up, and we know it. But we also want a place to belong, to be known. To us, ugly reality beats fake beauty any day. Perfection is a standard no one can meet.

But many of us grew up in homes and churches where image management was king. As a Christian, it was your goal to convince others of how spiritual you were. Reality was irrelevant. Perception was everything.

When this happens, little attention is given to actual hurt or doubt. Forced smiles cover up deep-seated pain and struggle. Jesus, the Bible, and prayer are the answers to every question.

As a student I once attended a church service with a guest speaker who was "famous." Eager to hear his remarks, I listened intently. He was a dynamic speaker, sure to connect with a new audience and exposit God's Word in a fresh way.

What followed was nothing less than a slew of self-glorifying stories filled with encounters and relationships with other "famous" people. I don't remember a single Scripture ever being read. All attention was given to his past ministry success and how he led with power and strength. The local church sat at his feet, soaking in everything.

I walked away completely disgusted. This was name-dropping and narcissism on a level few reach. Possibly more devastating was the church's response. They loved it. In stereotypical fashion, this Christian leader presented a version of Christianity that led to ministry success and material acquisition. And he wasn't even part of the prosperity gospel crowd.

Good intentions abounding, we have received a faith that values perception over reality. Mature Christians need to have their life in order. Mature Christians need to look good on Sunday morning. My generation has been taught this set of values. But such an attitude does not validate our struggles, doubt, or frustration. We learned that life is about having everything together . . . or at least playing the part.

For us and our culture, this makes no sense.

REALLY, THAT'S YOUR PRAYER?

As a young believer, I was taught that small groups are the answer to true community and fellowship. Surely, a group of Bible-believing people coming together would create a space of honesty and truth. It's a simple way to grow in the context of community.

In my experience the Bible study usually works out pretty well: read the passage, answer the questions, and walk away with a goal for the next week. Where this model often falls apart is at prayer time.

Insert Jon Acuff. Writer, speaker, and blogger. The following is a description of what happens next and what causes us to question the value of Christian community.

Have you ever been in a small group with people that confess safe sins? Someone will say, "I need to be honest with everyone tonight. I need to have full disclosure and submit myself in honesty. Like ODB from the Wu-Tang Clan, I need to give it to you raw!" So you brace yourself for this crazy moment of authenticity and the person takes a deep breath and says . . . "I haven't been reading my Bible enough."

Ugh, you, dirty, dirty sinner. I'm not even sure I can be in a small group with you any more. Not reading your Bible enough, that is disgusting. And then once he's gone someone else will catch the safe sin bug too and will say, "I need to be real too. I haven't been praying enough."

Two of you in the same room? Wow, freak shows! I can barely stand it.

But what happens when people start confessing safe sins is that everyone else in the room starts concealing thir real junk. I mean if I was surrounded by confessions like that in the eighth grade I would have instantly known I couldn't follow the "not reading my Bible enough" guy with my own story:

"Soooo, this weekend when it was snowing I told my parents I was going to the dump to sled but instead I was really just digging through a 200 foot mountain of warm trash looking for pornography." And the same principle would have applied to me in my late 20s. I wouldn't have been honest sharing my struggles with Internet porn if everyone else confessed their "safe enough for small group" sins.

And that sucks. It sucks that as broken as we all are, as desperate as we all are for a Savior, we feel compelled to clean ourselves up when we get around each other.

But this blog has taught me something unbelievable. If I stop writing tomorrow, this will be the lesson I cling to the most.

When you go first, you give everyone in your church or your community or your small group or your blog, the gift of going second.

It's much harder to be first. No one knows what's off limits yet and you're setting the boundaries with your words. You're throwing yourself on the honesty grenade and taking whatever fall out that comes with it. Going second is so much easier. And the ease only grows exponentially as people continue to share. But it has to be started somewhere. Someone has to go first and I think it has to be us.

We're called to give the gift of second to the people in our lives. To live the truth, to share the truth, to be the truth.

Let's give the gift of going second.[1]

Life and faith are not perfect. Whether it's sin or doubt, we struggle. We are all sinners in need of grace; not just for grace when we say "the prayer" but grace every day.

Sometimes I think the older we get as Christians, the more our theology can be distorted. For a believer who has known Christ for years, it is easy to acquire a sense of entitlement. You serve in the church, you are faithful to your small group, and you attend Sunday school. In a sense, you've arrived. You deserve God's grace. You've earned His favor. You've hit the mark.

I believe this mindset is not just possible but probable.

Why? Because the result of this attitude is pride. That pride then produces astronomical levels of rule-following. Self-righteousness and judgment quickly follow.

My generation has been frustrated and hurt by a Christian community and subculture that sometimes values perfection over faith. And it makes sense—our struggles are often not heard or welcome. Instead of grace being the common thread, the church has replaced it with moral and religious standards.

Many times we experience doubt or struggle with sin, yet we feel alienated from the church. We know the standard expected of "Christians" and we've fallen short. Like something unclean, no longer worthy of God or His church, we are ignored. This usually continues until we can "clean up" our lives enough to return.

But isn't that the gospel? Sinners redeemed by grace in order to extend grace? Shouldn't the church be seeking those people?

Michael Frost, author of *Exiles: Living Missionally in a Post-Christian Culture*, does well in describing this experience in the church. He talks about the millennials as a generation who have a "built-in, shockproof" detector for dishonesty and pretense. This awareness, cultivated by our generation's culture, leads us to see the inauthentic show often being put on by the church.

He goes on to speak about the alienation felt by audiences when pastors and worship leaders speak with overly spiritual language consisting of "hyper-real images and unlikely expectations." "Public Christian discourse seems to regularly concern itself with happy Christian families, answered prayers, and parables with an obvious moral inserted in the punch line." Later in the chapter he continues, "Perhaps there are many shiny, happy people in the church, but those of us who aren't shiny and don't feel perpetually happy eventually develop a strong sense of alienation. We're not able to play the game with any sense of integrity."[2]

A friend of mine, also a millennial, expressed a similar sentiment. He described the church as always having a "perpetual focus on joy and happiness." As someone who has experienced Christian community in Bible college, he talks about the constant pressure to be happy. With that focus, much of Christianity is centered on moralism and emotion rather than faith. This veneer of a perfect life has little room for doubts.

As a generation, we are frustrated at the language the church uses to express faith. Preachers and teachers who use perfect stories about "God showing up" don't often seem to acknowledge their struggles with faith. As a generation of people who speak their mind, and yearn for what is true, we cannot match the perfection presented in church.

And we question whether any of it is even real.

Anne Lamott, in her book *Bird by Bird*, talks about the necessity of writing truthfully. As she narrates the plot and develops characters, her constant focus is on describing what is real. She warns young writers of creating characters devoid of humanness. "They shouldn't be too perfect; perfect means shallow and unreal and fatally uninteresting."[3]

As a millennial, few things are as frustrating as inauthenticity, especially in relation to faith. Those who disguise or cover up what is real often find acceptance in the church. Yet this version of communal conformity does nothing to produce authentic faith.

We see this and it has caused many of us to walk away from Christian community and even the church. Living our faith outside the context of the church has become an attractive alternative.

ONE-DAY WORKWEEK

Much of the disillusionment I feel as a Christian is connected to the lack of holistic living present in the church today—be it work, family, or our interaction with unbelievers.

Case in point: the one-day workweek. It sounds like a new book on how to get rich, but more accurately it describes how the church often approaches faith. Faith becomes a segment of their life, set apart and holy, for Sundays (maybe Wednesdays too, if you're really dedicated).

This waffle-like approach to faith allows us to place our faith in one section, our work in another, and our hobbies in another. They are disconnected, without the ability to influence each other.

This is our experience in the church. Families go to worship, sing songs, listen to the sermon, and go home. For them, what continues throughout the rest of the week is anything but "church."

Matt Chambers blogged about his neighbor's experience with Christians who live a segmented life. After asking a neighbor why he never went to church, his neighbor said, "Matt, when I go to the strip club, sometimes there's another group of guys there. They say all the same things I say to the women, but during the day, they're in class studying to become pastors. Why do I need to believe what they believe when we all end up at the same place anyway?"[4]

If you grew up with that parent or pastor, I am sorry. Most of us didn't.

But my point, and the feeling shared by many of us, is that the church and Christian community often don't teach or exemplify a faith that affects your life outside of Sunday morning. And if they do, it's based off moralistic teaching of "perceived" spirituality and piety. This produces believers who simply are playing a game, not living out faith.

We see this as simply lip service. Spirituality should never be isolated to a two-hour slot each week. If faith can be scheduled and put on a checklist, it isn't faith.

YOU WANT ME TO DO WHAT?

Contrary to common thinking, a shallow version of Christianity is not compelling, relevant, or attractive to us. In fact, it's the thing that often drives us away from the church.

Living in Dallas, Texas, for two years gave me firsthand experience of the "Bible Belt." When friends in Chicago mention their frustration with cultural Christianity, I laugh to myself. They simply have no clue.

Everyone in Dallas goes to church. Every. Single. Person. It's a documented phenomenon.

This version of Christianity looks very different than that of LA or Seattle. In Dallas, it's cool to go to church. There is little negative social pressure against being "Christian." If you smoke pot, have tattoos, or are openly gay, you go to church. I knew people of each variety who went to Bible-believing churches and were even involved in small groups.

But in this type of "Christian" culture, the message and life of faith quickly falls to the lowest common denominator. Dallas could easily win the award for the most "Sunday-only" Christians.

As I lived there I was often asked what caused so many young believers to attend a particular megachurch. While most churches in Dallas are large, this church had an uncanny ability to attract our generation—and it wasn't flashy.

What I said was simple. Their version of Christianity is not cheap.

When you're drowning in a culture of Christianity that approves of everyone, people will look for more. Why? Because cheap Christianity, with low expectations, is virtually meaningless.

I would argue our generation desires a significant faith. We want a Sunday morning message to challenge us to something deeper than tutoring a student or cleaning up the neighborhood. Those things are important and should happen, but when disconnected from a compelling vision of God, they are simply acts of service.

Our morality and service should never be the motivation

for following Jesus. They must flow from deep, gut-wrenching truth about who God is, and what He deserves from us. Often the church presents a version of Christianity that awards a gold star to those who "serve" the most. If that's Christianity, I want out.

Compelling faith sees God as powerful and someone to be feared. Compelling faith knows we play a small part in relation to this world and will never deserve God's favor or grace. It realizes that, in light of His compassion and love, we are shown mercy.

Hearing a message on the nature, character, and power of God inspires us. We want to be challenged to love the unlovely, share our possessions with the poor, or give our lives to something that matters. That is what inspires our generation.

We don't want a watered-down version of God's Word. We don't accept a three-point checklist to complete this week. Token Christianity has nothing to do with following Jesus.

We want to start and end with God.

SOMETIMES I WANT TO FALL DOWN

Our generation is young. At the upper end, we've been walking this world for thirty years. That's not long, but it's not insignificant.

One of the greatest frustrations among our generation today is the church's overprotective culture. Whether in ministry or leadership, we are often told what can't be done. While it might indeed be true that what we want to do can't be done, the rejection simply turns us off to the church.

We are a generation with a unique set of gifts, values, and

experiences. We have grown up in a technological age unlike anything previous. We value the environment and are the most socially conscious generation in recent history. We are optimistic about the future and how God is working.

Not only that, we are dreamers. Every generation has thinkers and those who break through previous norms. I would argue our generation will set new standards on what is possible in arenas of church, parachurch, and business.

Charles Lee is CEO of Ideation, a unique group of innovators in the area of social good. He is described as an ideation strategist, networker, and compassionary. In a recent piece about millennials he wrote, "The creative implementation of innovative ideas is at an all-time high. Rapid advancements in technology and human networks have exponentially opened up new pathways to actualizing one's passions. Unlike in past centuries, people no longer need to wait for 'permission' from the established institutions to pursue a dream."[5]

We want the chance to step out on a limb for an idea, and if necessary, fail. What leads to frustration is when we're prevented from both.

Our generation is coming up with new ideas to engage culture, make disciples, share our faith, do missions, and take care of the poor. Many of these come out of a cultural background different than our parents'. Some ideas are more extreme than others.

Yet the church is not always a place that encourages this entrepreneurial spirit. Instead of empowering us, we are often pigeonholed into what is tried-and-true. We are told ministry is not the place to experiment with ideas. The church is a place for stewardship, and thus, proven methods for ministry are best.

The church is daily losing the most creative people to other arenas. Many of my friends have started businesses and nonprofits, seeking to care for the poor, feed the hungry, and further the kingdom. These are the same leaders and thinkers who were not welcomed by the church. Their ideas were too messy and untested. In the context of the church, they were seen as "too radical." So they leave, taking their passion and creativity into other arenas.

The church has yet to see the depth of this mistake.[6]

In light of our experience, we are often frustrated to the point where we simply want the freedom to mess up. Being "careful" is not an attractive option for us anymore. It is this fear-based guarding, which if left unaddressed, will bury everything once effective in the church. This type of restriction will not keep creative people in the church.

Ken and Deborah Loyd, pastors and authors, elaborate on this issue: "What if we older, more established church leaders who hold the authority, property, money, and other church resources were to hunt down eclectic, somewhat ragtag, young women and men, and give our power and stuff to them with the instruction, 'We choose you precisely because you are *not* like us. Here is your charge: Go after those who are seeking God. *Do not* copy our ways. *Do not* do what we have done. Innovate. Try. Fail. Succeed. Forge a new path. Build new kinds of churches and communities.'"[7]

Our generation needs encouragement and empowerment. We need to be affirmed in the new ways we are sharing the gospel and reaching those without Christ. We need opportunities to continue thinking and leading amidst a generation that despises "church services."

We need the freedom to fail.

2

Christians Don't Do That

When I tell someone I'm a Christian, I always get butter-flies. I'm not embarrassed about my beliefs or family background. No, those things are fine. I'm anxious and on edge because I don't know what type of Christianity they've encountered.

Let's be honest, the reputation of Christians in the world today is something of a patchwork. The world has been exposed to many flavors of Christianity. Some think old and faithful—Billy Graham. Some think rich and unethical—Benny Hinn. Others think homely and out of touch with reality—you know who I'm talking about. Still others are turned off by Christians vocally supporting a specific political party.

The landscape is broad and eclectic. Some Christians I'd have over for dinner any night. Others I'd like to avoid.

We all have to deal with the reputation and perception placed on us because of other "Christians." None of us start with a clean slate.

I DON'T WANT TO BE A "CHRISTIAN"

In 2007 David Kinnaman and Gabe Lyons wrote the book *unChristian.* It revealed to the church what non-Christians thought of Christians. Like someone removing a blindfold, many Christians were shocked by the research. Others couldn't understand why it had taken so long for the truth to come out.

Yet the aftershock that followed was even more devastating. Many Christians felt the same way about Christians.

Hypocritical.

Overemphasis on conversion.

Antihomosexual.

Sheltered.

Too political.

Judgmental.[1]

The church was finally awakened to its current reputation. And I felt embarrassed. Our generation felt embarrassed.

Maybe that was the goal.

THINK FOR YOURSELF

Growing up in the church does funny things to you. Add to that a conservative family and you're bound to have stories.

If I were to imagine a stereotypical Christian family, one thing would quickly surface: they are "Christian." Not only would they say they are Christians, you would see evidence everywhere.

Christian music. Christian movies. Christian school. Christian sports. Christian clothing. Christian books. Christian bumper stickers. Christian video games. Christian everything.

My generation grew up in "Christian" homes to the hilt. Yet despite good motives, there were unintended results.

Two are apparent: (1) A lack of creativity. People slap

"Christian" labels on anything from Hollywood to Wal-Mart to make them acceptable. Case in point, the Christian version of YouTube, originally labeled "GodTube." (2) An overemphasis on morality. People choose morality rather than faith as the distinguishing mark of what makes them "Christian."

The Christian reputation is known for knockoffs, not originality. That is embarrassing to my generation and rightly so. It symbolizes our need to be known as "Christian," revealing roots of fear and insecurity. It also goes against the creative nature of our God.

Instead of copying this world and putting a Christian twist on it—let us create. This is the heartbeat of many entrepreneurs in our generation. It is a desire to innovate, solve problems, and infuse beauty into this world.

THE GOOD OL' DAYS

Two conversations often come up with older believers. First, they enjoy talking about the good ol' days when Christians were the moral majority. Second, they lament how the world is headed to hell in a handbasket.

Personally, I find these conversations incredibly unhelpful. What remains obvious to all—we are young. As someone who is unable to rent a car without additional fees, I acknowledge my limits.

However, my generation views the future with optimism. When the conversation turns to the good ol' days, everyone under the age of sixty is left out of a moment of divine nostalgia—a time when Christian morals dominated the public square. Clearly, the glory years.

The conversation inevitably turns to the present state of affairs. Good luck to those who are young. If only we had lived during history's Christendom.

C. S. Lewis once coined the phrase "chronological snobbery." It refers to the erroneous argument that the thinking, art, or science of a previous time period is inferior simply because it occurred in the past. This is often applied to current generations, encouraging them to not look down upon their parents' way of doing things. Yet, I believe there is an additional application here if inversely applied.

Just because the past was good does not mean the future is doomed. And clearly the "Christian" culture of our parents and grandparents was flawed. If you're not convinced, keep reading.

Our generation is passionate about the gospel and has enormous hope for the future. I speak with peers often who have dreams of how God will work. Much is already happening.

Theologically, the gospel is as powerful today as it was at Pentecost or the Great Awakening. As long as God allows the world to continue, He has a plan. To throw in the towel at any point would be unbiblical. In the same way, we should not be afraid of the world simply because it's changing.

Granted, the world is not the same as it was. Christian morals are not held as they once were. But that is not the end of God's work. In fact, I would argue, as many others do, that this is exactly what the church needs. It is this shift that could shake the church from its indifference and apathy.

I think we are a part of a generation that has incredible hope. Hope for the gospel. Hope for God's kingdom. Hope for healing. Hearing the previous generation talk about the future as dismal is annoying and hurtful. Leaders are emerging from our generation with conviction and courage. Believers are living for Christ with new-found relevance and authenticity. As America grows less Christian in its culture, faith is being refined. Don't allow the church to look down on our generation. God is still at work.

JESUS WASN'T REPUBLICAN

As a millennial, it is often embarrassing to hear the religious connections made to politics. Growing up in the evangelical faith, we've all heard the right-wing, conservative agenda set forth in the name of Christianity.

Too often the church has narrowed its focus to specific issues. For example, the church is pro-life. The church is against gay marriage. Political conversation has rarely extended beyond these "hot-button" issues.

We as a generation have rejected this approach. While we are engaged in issues and politics, we are careful in how we apply our faith. Jesus isn't a Republican.[2] The church cannot act as if He's on our side and against all liberals. Our generation is doing our best to separate issues of faith and policy.

Instead of holding dogmatic allegiance to a political party, we are pursuing broader change in culture. As noted by others, policy is always a result of practice. Starting with cultural change will always exceed the impact of any political protest.

Damon of Athens once wrote, "Give me the songs of a nation and it does not matter who writes its laws." Instead of protesting issues with banners and crowds, we are seeking to live out our faith in the community.

Our generation still holds many of the values of our parents. Pro-life remains an important issue in our minds. Yet our generation has taken the conversation deeper as we look at the connected issues. This has led to a greater emphasis on the church's involvement in adoption, caring for the elderly, and serving in pregnancy centers—all issues related to the sanctity of life.

Our tone is also significant. We understand the value of nonabrasive dialogue. Growing up in Christian communities where Democrats were often treated as hell-bound sinners is not something we are proud of. We want to engage in helpful conversations that value each party.

We are changing how we interact with politics in the public square. Party affiliation no longer fulfills our Christian responsibility. Authentic living and thoughtful response have replaced political affiliation.

THEY'RE STILL PEOPLE

When *unChristian* raised the issue of homosexuality, no one was surprised. To label Christians "antihomosexual" seemed a bit harsh to some. Many would argue it was a fair description of the church's reputation.

Kinnaman quotes Peter, a thirty-four-year-old, saying, "Many people in the gay community don't seem to have issues with Jesus but rather with those claiming to represent him today. It's very much an 'us-versus-them' mentality, as if a war has been declared. Of course each side thinks the other fired the opening shot."[3]

The Christian reputation, established primarily by the previous generation, has been known to show judgment and doctrinal separation. Few would describe this conversation as loving.

While I will explore this more in a later chapter, the church has lost many of their relationships with the gay community. This is often the result of the harsh tone in which homosexuality is labeled as "sin."

Resulting interactions with those in the gay community have become awkward, stiff, and anything but welcoming. As a millennial, I want nothing to do with that reputation.

The church has struggled to know how to welcome gays into their community. The moment a gay or lesbian couple walks into a church lobby, they are often met with stares, whispering, and avoidance. It is as if lepers have invaded the premises of the church. Few are interested in introductions or friendship.

While stories of outward hatred toward homosexuals are many, I believe the church's most common failure is avoidance. The awkwardness linked to relationships within the gay community shows the church's inability to connect. This is a reputation our generation wants to repair.

As a generation entering the church and world, we have a negative reputation in the gay community because we're Christians. While much has been done to inflict those wounds, I believe there are many working to heal relationships and our reputation. Nathan Albert is one of those people. Here is a section from his blog:

I hugged a man in his underwear. I think Jesus would have too.

I spent the day at Chicago's Pride Parade. Some friends and I, with The Marin Foundation, wore shirts with "I'm Sorry" written on it. We had signs that said, "I'm sorry that Christians judge you," "I'm sorry the way churches have treated you," "I used to be a bible-banging homophobe, sorry." We wanted to be an alternative Christian voice from the protestors that were there speaking hate into megaphones.

What I loved most about the day is when people "got it." I loved watching people's faces as they saw our shirts, read the signs, and looked back at us. Responses were incredible. Some people blew us kisses, some hugged us, some screamed thank you. A couple ladies walked up and said we were the best thing they had seen all day. I wish I had counted how many people hugged me. One guy in particular softly said, "Well, I forgive you."

Watching people recognize our apology brought me to tears many times. It was reconciliation personified.

My favorite though was a gentleman who was dancing on a float. He was dressed solely in white underwear and had a pack of abs like no one else. As he was dancing on the float, he noticed us and jokingly yelled, "What are you sorry for? It's pride!" I pointed to our signs and watched him read them.

Then it clicked.

Then he got it.

He stopped dancing. He looked at all of us standing there. A look of utter seriousness came across his face. And as the float passed us he jumped off of it and ran towards us. In all his sweaty beautiful abs of steel, he hugged me and whispered, "thank you."

Before I had even let go, another guy ran up to me, kissed me on the cheek, and gave me the biggest bear hug ever. I almost had the wind knocked out of me; it was one of those hugs.

This is why I do what I do. This is why I will continue to do what I do. Reconciliation was personified.[4]

The gay community does not need our dogmas, creeds, or evaluation of their lives. Believe me, they know where we stand. Instead, they need our love. They're people made in the image of God, and should be treated as such. We need to educate our churches on how to welcome them into our communities.

We need to relearn how to relate to those living the homosexual lifestyle. Pietistic compulsion to share our convictions does not lead to relationship or reconciliation. It is only out of the overflow of relationship that we can lovingly share our heart. Yet, few Christians have ever said, "That's my friend," before they say, "That's sin."

This is a gross misrepresentation of Christ.

I believe Jesus modeled a better way in Luke 7 when He allows a prostitute to wash His feet—an act that, in His society, would bring Him shame. His focus was not on the doctrinal evaluation of this woman's life. Rather, He showed her love and forgiveness. He was more concerned about the woman than His reputation.

I believe individuals and the church often fail because they are fearful of their reputation. What would happen if someone saw them with a gay couple? What would others think if their community group welcomed a lesbian? Image management rises to the surface and trumps all. Biblical love is set aside, replaced by insecure self-protection.

I believe it should be our generation's aim to forever change the church's reputation from one of judgment to one of love.

I DON'T KNOW

We are skeptical. Growing up in the church, we were taught a theology that gave concrete answers to every situation. True faith was assumed and questions were not always welcome.

Yet doubt and cynicism mark much of who we are. Growing up in the '80s and '90s gave us reasons to question perceived truth. CEOs of Fortune 500 companies were scamming millions. Well-known pastors and priests were charged with sex abuse and adultery. Much of what we experienced fell short of what was promised.

And so we doubted. Some of us doubted our faith; others, our churches; others, our families. We doubted their love for us, their motivations, their stories, and their advice. Talking heads no longer meant anything to us. We often questioned whether their motives were pure. We wondered if their motives were based on greed, lust, or power.

While some of us were accepted as we struggled through

these doubts, many were uninvited to the church. This often occurred when our doubts concerned faith.

A friend of mine felt dismissed after he had questioned faith and theology too much. While studying at an academic institution, he was reprimanded for examining liberal theology and their answers to his questions.

My experience was similar, as many classes would read liberal theology with the goal and only option of condemning it. This type of theological molding leads us to question whether the church is a safe place to express doubts.

Timothy Keller puts it well in saying,

> A faith without some doubts is like a human body without any antibodies in it. People who blithely go through life too busy or indifferent to ask hard questions about why they believe as they do will find themselves defenseless against either the experience of tragedy or the probing questions of a smart skeptic. A person's faith can collapse almost overnight if she has failed over the years to listen patiently to her own doubts, which should only be discarded after long reflection.[5]

Doubt *should* be a part of our faith. Without it, we are simply accepting truth as fact, not thinking for ourselves. For those of our generation who have had doubts and continue to doubt—don't stop until you get your questions answered.

To be rejected because of doubt should cause us to leave that context, not our doubts.

As mentioned earlier, fear can often creep into the church

when doubts are expressed. Fear that your doubts will lead to liberal faith. Fear that traditional beliefs will no longer be held. Yet, this fear often pushes doubters away from the church.

Just as those who doubt should continue to explore their doubts, those with faith should continue in faith. Yet often this is not the case.

For those participating in and leading the church, faith is vital. This kind of faith trusts that God is active and powerful. It believes that those who are searching will be led by the Holy Spirit toward truth, not error. It even causes those in leadership to explore their own doubts instead of portraying Superman-like faith that never wavers.

To those who have been separated from the church because of doubt: keep searching and questioning. To those who have remained silent, quietly struggling with their faith: be honest and open. Talk through your questions. Leave room for uncertainty.

The following is advice from an agnostic friend—someone I admire for his honesty.

Allow God to defend Himself. So often we live as if God and His truth rely solely on us. God has called His community to live as truth and light, but His truth will not cease if people doubt. Instead of making God's truth and reputation our responsibility, let us live honestly and openly about our faith.

Let those with faith spread it widely.

Let those who doubt be welcomed and loved.

3

Bringing Back Christian America

Right now, our generation is exploring what it means to be "in the world but not of the world." Following our culture's values, we are less judgmental, more tolerant, and will virtually accept anyone as a friend. The issues come when the church judges our actions, suggesting we have compromised our "witness" for Christ.

As noted already, we are pursuing Christ in ways different from those before us. Our desire is to befriend believers and unbelievers alike. The church often condemns this approach to deeply engage in the world. It is viewed as "too worldly." Yet their criticism doesn't stop with how we interact with unbelievers.

UNDER A ROCK

As our generation has grown up in the conservative, evangelical church, we have been surrounded by a call for a Christian America. This value was epitomized in the Moral Majority started by Jerry Falwell.

The goal of this group was to bring conservative morals

to America. This passion was clear as they would often fight political battles to bring back "Christian" values. "Culture Wars" quickly became the term used to describe the struggle between Christians and secular culture.

We grew up during these years. Our parents were often the ones fighting against anything "secular" or "pagan." Lines were drawn, standards were established, and the church seemed determined to not lose their children to the world.

Because of this, many of us experienced an overwhelming sense that the world was evil. Anything not specifically "Christian" was suspect. Pastors would often teach this value system, condemning popular movies and music deemed offensive. In order to follow Christ, families were urged to protect their children from all types of immorality. In many ways, this was the church's stand for Christ.

THE THIRD PLACE

We don't want Christians to be our only friends.

Since childhood, the majority of our parents chose our activities, events, and places to hang out. As described in the previous chapter, this form of guidance focused on making every aspect of life "Christian."

Some of you lived this life. You grew up in a Christian family, you went to church, you went to Christian school, and most of your friends were Christian. This was the "community" preached about in church, and the examples were clear. Safe places included a church friend's house and athletic teams coached by Christians. A Christian bubble guarded against the world's negative influence.

Many of us were shaped through this period, concluding that either our family had a beautiful, safe life or we had completely missed the gospel. Either way, we were shown a version of Christianity safely removed from the world and unbelievers.

Michael Frost talks about this pattern of living in terms of the "third place." We all have our first two spaces, home and work. The third place is the area of our life where we spend time after home and work. In our experience, it was usually a Christian third space.

After explaining that most Christians don't have time for third places that engage unbelievers, Frost writes, "The reason for this is that for most Christians their church has become their third place. Their churches soak up every bit of their spare time. All their social networks revolve around church."[1]

For most of the world, third places are cafés, pubs, and bars. That's where people go for informal gatherings, a sense of community, and a place to unwind with friends. Every day, they participate in these spaces.

But for many of us, we were either protected from or too busy to engage with unbelievers in these places. Looking back now, we see the devastation that a busy Christian life can have on our faith. Instead of reaching out to the world with hope, we focused inwardly on places that are safe and "Christian."

Our generation is changing this mindset. We see the third place as a primary way to connect with those outside the church. Instead of having sporadic "evangelistic" outings to such places, we choose to live with unbelievers and develop friendships without obvious intentions to "convert" them. This leads us to spend time at coffee shops and bars, providing the opportunity to develop relationships with those outside the church.

Yet often this approach leads to further judgment as the church views this lifestyle as too connected to the world. They ask, "How are you different? How will they know you're not like them?"

Those questions show that differences and misunderstandings still exist. More on this in chapter 5.

BEING "DIFFERENT"—PART 1

We have seen one way to be different.

Christ told us to be "in the world but not of it." But what does that mean?

Our parents answered this question clearly: our morality.

In a response to the moral decay of the '60s and '70s, many of our boomer parents and pastors took a firm stand on moral issues. They said Christians were different because of our morals. We don't smoke. We don't swear. We don't go to the bar or drink beer. We don't watch R-rated movies. We don't wear bikinis. We don't, we don't, we don't . . .

Christians are often known for a religion concerned with what we don't do. Why? Because that separates us from a secular and evil world. Separation became the standard for Christian community, as it has for so many generations before us. It shows believers what it means to follow Christ in a Christless culture.

This is a huge frustration to our generation. Yes, we know

the gospel can offend. Yet too often we have seen the church offend unbelievers for the wrong reasons. This is often because Christians are so intent on showing the world that they are "different."

Our generation knows God expects the church to be different from the world. Clearly we should abstain from immorality, love our enemies, and share Christ as the only way to God. Our problem comes when the church substitutes lesser, moralistic or cultural preferences for these biblical distinctives.

Abstaining from alcohol, refraining from tattoos, and avoiding cigars are all standards commonly held by our parents' generation. While these may be appropriate preferences for individuals, they should not be held as corporate expectations in the church. Instead, many in my generation view these as areas of freedom for the believer to discern personally.

Our generation is often judged when we choose to exercise our freedom in these areas.

In the experience of many in the church, faith has been equated with a set of rules. This is not a boomer problem, this is a human problem. The church has turned life and spirituality into a list. They have laid out expectations and looked for the requirements to attain "godliness." Those who are spiritual pass the test.

Think church attendance and quiet times.

Growing up, our generation did not understand the impact this type of faith would have on our lives. For me, it worked for twenty-two years. Then it all fell apart.

PASTORAL TRAINING

Attending seminary was one of the driest times of my life spiritually.

Having spent four years studying at Moody Bible Institute, I jumped into a master's program with little thought. What followed were a number of intro courses in theology, biblical studies, and spiritual formation. Moody 2.0.

After my first semester, I simply couldn't play the game any longer. I struggled with the evangelical values the church had passed on to me. Real life had hit and it didn't match up with my "Christian" structure.

Every situation since childhood had fit into my little box. Practically, philosophically, and theologically, I had an answer for each question. Life made sense. The Bible was clear. The future was mapped out.

I'm not sure what happened, but I started to question all that I had been taught. Why? Because life and theology and God no longer made sense. At least the way it once did.

Holding on to morality as my foundation for faith had left me stranded. Being "good" and following the behavioral expectations of the church brought nothing but frustration and legalism. My understanding of life and faith had been challenged, and instead of responding with answers, I chose to ask more questions.

BEING "DIFFERENT"—PART 2

Many of us have rejected the church's previous standards for being different from the world. Some of us are comfortable being around alcohol and even having a drink ourselves.

We socialize with unbelievers, not seeking to remain only in our Christian bubbles. Some have even used tattoos to help express their faith and dedication to Christ. We are sensitive to not offend unbelievers. This is not because we don't want to attach ourselves to Christ but rather we have seen the church take a stand for the wrong reasons. In contrast to that, we want to be "normal" while following Jesus.

This type of nonoffensive living is expressed in Carl Medearis's book *Speaking of Jesus: The Art of Non-Evangelism*. Medearis explains a new paradigm that influences how many in our generation live as believers.

He refers to the church's approach to evangelism as a war. Team Jesus vs. Team Anti-Jesus. The church is on one side while the rest of the world and its religions are on the other. Our goal is to win by getting the most on our side. We cannot fail our fearless leader, Jesus.

Medearis writes about how this idea is deadly to following and sharing Jesus. Unbelievers are not our enemies simply because they don't follow Jesus.[2]

Instead of an "us vs. them" mentality, we should simply follow Jesus. Living with this value, in turn, refocuses our interaction and relationship with unbelievers.

BUSINESS AS USUAL

Growing up in the church gives many people an interesting view of business. One can think of business as a secular form of making money, but below the calling of a pastor or missionary. In this view, a believer's life at work is disconnected from the work of Christ and the church.

Our generation does not associate with this view. In its place, we are responding by connecting Christ and business in unique ways. Starting with a passion for Christ, we are dreaming of ways to meet needs, provide responsible services, and serve our communities. Yet, they are far less "Christian" than the church has known in the past.

Kammok is a perfect example.[3]

Started by a friend from seminary, Kammok is an outdoor adventure brand for the socially conscious adventurer. It is their mission to connect the outdoor community with the life-changing adventure of caring for people.

With the sale of each lightweight camping hammock, they donate a treated mosquito net or health education to a family in Africa through Malaria No More. Along with helping to prevent malaria, they support other nonprofits who are working to provide sustainable development and health-related initiatives to those in need.

Yet, in spite of a foundation of Christian values propelling Kammok, they are not a "Christian" company. They will never stitch John 3:16 on their product tags. Their website will not contain information about Scripture, doctrine, or following Jesus. These are intentional choices made with the goal of sharing Christ's love without branding the company "Christian."

Many millennial businesses and nonprofits are following this example, choosing to avoid the Christian label to avoid the baggage and exclusivity connected to the name. While faith in Christ alone is exclusive, business does not need to mirror this distinction. There is a third way to live missionally without titling a for-profit business as Protestant.

In our experience, avoiding the Christian label has led to many more opportunities for both business and mission. This is a reaction to the church's previous separation from everything not Christian. We see God calling us to reach people, connect with others, and do our best to give grace and love.

Business is an amazing way to follow Christ and spread His love. Caring for people by providing products and services allows us to build relationships. Friendships like these are a huge reason businesses like Kammok are formed. They see our obligation in this world as extending past doctrinal propositions and evangelistic tracts. What hurts is that we often feel judged by the church when we are not explicitly sharing the gospel through our business or everyday life.

God has placed us here to live faithfully and love others, even if we live and love in unconventional ways.

4

Avoiding the "Bar Scene"

Thirty years ago, the American evangelical church member would never dream of being caught in a bar. Today, churches are being planted there. Amid the social environment found in pubs, we see opportunities to express the hope of Christ to those who enjoy a pint as they talk about life. This is new to the evangelical church and an opportunity to engage culture and unbelievers.

Christian freedom has long been a debated topic of conversation in the church. Like grace, freedom is often used and abused. Keeping this fact in mind, our generation is reconsidering the views often taught in evangelical churches.

The church has avoided grey issues for years, seemingly to remain safe from harm. We want to enter into those areas to connect with unbelievers and enjoy life. In pursuing mission, we often leave the Christian subculture to engage the world.

CHILD OF GOD

I have a tattoo.

Yes, it's in Greek. But it isn't a fashion statement.

Being raised in the church, I felt a lot of expectations. Add "pastor's kid" on to that and those pressures only increased. I never remember someone coming up to me with a list of rules to follow, at least not a physical list. But despite not having a tangible copy to carry around, I knew what was required.

In my early twenties I came to a place of desperation. I couldn't follow the list anymore. I no longer cared about fitting into the traditional molds of "pastor," "leader," and "mature." Everything they represented now awakened frustration, not respect.

At age twenty-three I allowed a stranger to etch the Greek words τέκνον θεοῦ into my side. While meaningless to the average person, those two words have enormous significance for me. Literally translated, they mean "Child of God."

At the depth of my frustration, I realized I could no longer live to please people. I had spent most of my young life consumed with pursuing their applause.

This tattoo signified a change in my life. For two decades I lived in the shadow of those above me, always seeking to copy them and their standards. Christianity had become a game. Follow the rules, play the part, and you'll be accepted.

I did everything I could to become that person. And when I looked back over years of jumping the hoops, I felt empty.

In the ideal timing, God taught me this truth:

You are My child.

Before any human family, church body, or Christian formula. You are Mine.

And because you are Mine, I give you freedom to live for Me. Not for people.

LIFE FOR CHRIST

Since that day I have felt an unbelievable sense of peace—a comfort and rest, freeing me from the anxiety of living up to others' standards.

Living as a child of God has freed me to live for Him, despite the world's opposition—and the church's. My priorities have been realigned, with devotion to God taking the first slot. Connected to that devotion is an empowerment to live as God designed me. It might not look like how my parents live. It might go against the typical "Christian" mold. Those things, which once held me back, are no longer the decision makers.

My greatest desire and adventure is to follow Jesus Christ. He has called me to love Him and love people. Others' opinions no longer determine my direction. Will I pursue godly counsel? Of course. Will I allow others' influence to control my life or values? Never.

And so I step forward each day, knowing I can live without regret as I follow Him—whatever that may bring.

A NEW PERSPECTIVE

Jesus introduced a new way of living.

Many in the first century followed pagan gods who demanded absolute obedience. Religion brought up memories of obligatory good works, with the constant threat of punishment. Life was focused on measuring up to a standard. For those who lived according to this authority, Jesus' teaching was a splash of fresh water. He replaced religious chains with openhanded grace.

Jesus came to remove the religious system. Up to this

point, humanity knew nothing but rules. Stepping into human flesh, Jesus rewrote everyone's expectations. And He did it with grace and love. Instead of requiring religious piety, He gave freedom. And faith was His primary aim. He wanted followers who held deep trust as their foundation, not social or political conformity.

The millennial generation is living with a fresh sense of freedom. While this openness certainly touches on topics of Christian freedom, it's broader than just that. It's a mindset, an attitude.

The world has changed, and the rules from 1990 no longer apply. In fact, they often make little sense to our generation. In light of technology, globalization, and a host of other factors, our generation lives life differently.

Part of that life is freedom. Often, freedom to be different.

That's why we can choose to wear our grandparents' style of clothing, get a tattoo sleeve, work part-time as a freelance artist, or travel the world for months at a time. Norms don't match those of previous generations. Some would argue there are no norms.

Culture has shifted in the last ten years and the world is a very different place. The business world is starting to understand this and is working to accommodate. What's discouraging to many in our generation is the church's belated response.

As a generation, we differentiate ourselves by being ourselves. Weird is cool and quirky is encouraged. Anything mainstream is, well, no longer mainstream. People don't want to fit into molds. In its place, we combine interests and personality into a distinctive mosaic.

It is this freedom that encourages us to look different than our parents. For many of us, we don't question whether we should copy the church or its leaders. We expect to create something new. We expect to look and live differently.

It only follows, then, that we would view Christian freedom in a new light.

THE CHURCH AND FREEDOM

Growing up, our generation has often been frustrated by the dogmatism associated with Christian freedom. As some of us make certain lifestyle choices, we often experience judgment from the church and its leaders. While alcohol is usually the most visible topic, this conversation extends to issues like tattoos, smoking, piercing, and other areas of Christian freedom.

The church has often taught that issues of Christian freedom are permissible for believers, yet not preferable. Many of us knew that participating in these things would likely result in disapproval from our parents and pastors.

Another common view held in the church relates to the need to be "safe" from the world. When issues of Christian freedom are addressed, they are often talked about as dangerous or unnecessary. This is where the conversation usually ends.

As our generation desires to explore our freedom, this often causes the church to look down on us. We are judged as "less spiritual" by choosing to drink. While not stated explicitly, this is often implied. Body language, indirect remarks, and approval of those who abstain are a few ways this occurs.

In our experience, the church does not always provide

a place for adequate dialogue. Instead, leadership often discourages the practice of freedom, often out of fear that the congregation would abuse the privilege. This has led many in our generation to rebel against the church's teaching.

Having spent many Sundays in the pew, we often heard an overreactive teaching concerning the weaker brother. Abstinence was often the moral conclusion. These messages provided hypothetical stories told in a way that produced fear of ever violating Paul's warning. For example, if some weak brother, somewhere, knew we were drinking . . . they might stumble.

Therefore, we should never drink again.

In our experience, spiritual red tape keeps many people from exploring Christian freedom. As we grew up in the church, we often felt a fence, keeping us from straying too far. Yet we didn't feel love or grace during those moments. Topics like drinking were addressed with a different tone—one filled with anxiety and fear.

Sometimes I wonder if the drinking and tattoos of today are the dancing and movie theatres of our grandparents' day.

ENGAGING OTHERS

Our choice to practice or not practice Christian freedom affects our ability to relate to people. Whether Christian or not, many people choose to drink or tattoos for social reasons. It gives them a place to go after work—something to do as they unwind and process the day. In all honesty, it is a simple way to connect with others. We see this as an opportunity, not a danger.

Recently I heard a story on this topic from a friend. We'll call him Jeff.

After graduating from college, Jeff moved back to his hometown and was working at a church. One of his brothers still lived in the area but wasn't too interested in Jesus. With little in common, talking seemed awkward. Especially surrounding faith.

In an effort to do something together, Jeff offered his brother a cigar and beer one night.

While neither drinking nor smoking communicated the gospel, it built their friendship and became a weekly tradition. Up to this point his brother only thought of Jeff as a Christian who followed a bunch of rules and tried to be "holy." Jeff engaged his brother over a beer and was able to connect. Now their conversation routinely comes back to faith and Scripture.

As a generation, we are passionate about relating to those who are without Christ. Often this does not take place in the church but in the bar or at a party. In light of the Christian freedom presented in Scripture, we have done much to connect with people previously outside the church's reach. Yet, few things have brought more severe judgment from the church upon our generation.

It is moments like these that make us want to leave the church.

As a resident assistant in college, I had numerous conversations with other student leaders surrounding this topic. While my views were still being shaped, I heard a constant theme from my peers: drinking is not a big deal. In fact, many planned to enjoy a good drink after walking across the stage at graduation. For some, having one drink might seem insignificant. Yet for many Christian colleges, organizations, and churches, this may be unexplored ground.

JESUS AND PHARISEES

I've often thought about Jesus' response to the Pharisees in the Gospels. No one would argue they were religious leaders well-versed in the Torah and morally spotless. Yet, it is also clear that Jesus opposed them and their legalism.

As I look at the church today, it sometimes looks similar to the Pharisees of Jesus' day. In sermons, pastors will often label Pharisees as the extremist legalists of their day. They continue by identifying another group within Christianity and calmly assuring their church of their safety from such hypocrisy. This lack of self-reflection has deadly potential. It gives a false sense of comfort when legalism may actually be present.

The Pharisees commonly referred to these rules as a "fence around the law." The rules were detailed regulations placed on spiritual communities to guard against transgressing the clear biblical commandments. Yet, Jesus condemned this practice in the Pharisees' community. In Matthew 23 He opposes the legalistic standards the Pharisees had developed. Our generation has responded similarly as we have refused the extra standards commonly found in the church.

Our generation is choosing to practice Christian freedom differently. There is less fear surrounding alcohol or tattoos. While wisdom is paramount, I believe we've broken through many legalistic tendencies rooted in the church. Yet subtly we have been pushed out of churches and leadership roles because of this issue.

While legalism is rarely blatant (at least in most churches), we should not think it has disappeared. Christian freedom leaves no room for prejudice based on personal preference. Just like the Pharisees, additional rules are often instilled in churches and used to create layers of acceptance and authority in the church.

For us to faithfully lead the church tomorrow, we need to understand Jesus' teaching against the Pharisees and confront the legalism of our day. Whatever our personal preference in regard to alcohol or tattoos, we should oppose anyone seeking to set standards above another. The church was not founded to establish extrabiblical morals for believers. When this happens, they are rehearsing an ancient mistake exemplified in the Pharisees.

FREEDOM TOWARD MATURITY

Hebrews 5:11–14 is a call to spiritual maturity. The writer addresses believers who were still spiritual babies, rebuking them for remaining infants in their faith when they should now be mature. Instead of leading the church, they were still in need of others to feed them the spiritual basics. One mark of this immaturity was a lack of discernment "to distinguish good from evil" (Hebrews 5:14b).

Without personal experience, my knowledge of parenting is as follows: infants and young children need concrete rules to develop a foundational understanding of how to behave.

Teenagers need continued expectations, yet with greater freedom to learn and to develop personal values. Adults need advice, yet have complete freedom to live according to their individual preferences.

The church has often failed at parenting our generation in the area of Christian freedom.

Many from our generation grew up with black-and-white rules regarding Christian freedom. While many in the church today practice freedom in regard to drinking or tattoos, the public perception and teaching often remains dogmatic. It is clear that the church's conservative stance still influences its language and response to issues like these.

We understand freedom is necessary to develop maturity. Just as Hebrews says it, maturity has the ability "to distinguish good from evil." This ability to discern is only acquired when freedom is extended. Parenting adults with rules only leads to legalistic control or outright rebellion.

It is this lack of freedom that leaves us frustrated and disillusioned.

SPEAKING OF JESUS

In the end, we want to follow Jesus.

As Paul opposed the legalistic leaders in Romans, he did so with one intention: to give people the freedom Jesus offers.

Roman gods demanded obedience from their followers, often with the threat of punishment. As Paul teaches the believers a new way, he is lifting that judgment. He wants the church to know Jesus does not hold those standards of judgment and condemnation. He came to offer grace and love, not law. Believers do not have to live under constant threat of punishment. They do not have strict rules to observe to please the gods. We serve a God who has already accepted us. Many people in the church come from backgrounds in legalism. And often, this is attractive to them. They understand the rules and do their best to follow them. Yet, Jesus opposes this rule-based faith. He desires a faith that is sensitive in the grey areas and a lifestyle of worship, influenced by love, not obligation.

While our generation is young in our understanding of freedom, we understand Jesus' message of grace. The church at times tends to value legalism over freedom. We want to help curb that tradition and bring back a healthier response.

If so, then Christian freedom can be restored to what it is . . . a gift from God.

5

Are You a Supralapsarian?

Alienation from the church is a common experience in our generation, often because of doctrine. No, we do not deny the deity or humanity of Christ, salvation by grace through faith, or Christ's imminent return. We agree on those things.

The difference between our generation and the church is our priorities. The conservative, evangelical church has been known to boldly and publicly state their doctrinal views for the world to hear. Few would have to guess what our parents think on these issues. They are loud and clear.

Our generation avoids that approach. We've seen relationships damaged beyond repair by the church's emphasis on doctrine. Yet our hesitancy to share our convictions often results in the church condemning us.

One further thought before moving on: the leaders in our generation do not value relationships as more important than doctrine. We understand the foundation that doctrine and theology provides for every believer. Yet we want to communicate doctrine in a way that is sensitive to people.

RELATIONSHIPS AND DOCTRINE

Our generation has made a dynamic shift in the values handed down from our parents. In light of the deep-rooted connectivity of our generation, relationships are now king. This is due, in part, to the incredible impact of social media and the increased influence of youth culture. We start with people, often before doctrine.

The implications of such a shift are numerous.

To begin, we are far more tolerant than any previous generation. This is a natural result of valuing people. Our doctrinal differences no longer create the boundaries they once did. Our religious preferences lead to less segregation and more positive dialogue. As a whole, we seek to build relationships on our common interests, rather than bringing up controversial issues. We want to engage others personally before bridging into areas of theology or religion.

Some from the boomer generation, on the other hand, seem to value correct doctrine above all else. Creeds and theological propositions are paramount to staying on track. The church should hold on to the purity of the gospel, fending off anyone who would challenge its claims.

This philosophical difference has brought about concerns, and even accusations, on our generation. In light of our relational priority, many church leaders have questioned our commitment to orthodoxy. They often talk of our generation as being syncretistic. The line separating us from the world remains blurry, if not invisible in their eyes. Yet, we see many benefits to this change in thinking.

As our generation has entered the church as adults and

leaders, we have not met the church's expectations. Because of our value of "relationship before doctrine," the church has often wondered if we no longer share biblical convictions. This has led to frustration for us as we are written off as believers with little doctrinal interest.

TRUTH WITHOUT PEOPLE

The Christian reputation handed down to us is far from gracious toward those outside the faith. We have grown up watching doctrinal differences stunt relationships with unbelievers as the church blurts out their convictions. This usually occurs before there is any relational connection. Our generation is doing what we can to avoid that stereotype.

One of the areas where this has clearly shown up is with homosexuals. While this topic was covered earlier, it plays an important part in this conversation as well. In an effort to remain distinct from the world and not be mistaken as condoning the gay lifestyle, the church has often placed their doctrinal convictions at the forefront of relationships with homosexuals. This communicates anything but love and acceptance. "You can come to our church, just know that we think you're an abomination to God."

As a result, the church has, in some cases, managed to distance themselves from unbelievers. Some unbelievers seem to run from the church because of some unsaid prerequisite that they must hear out our doctrine before we can be friends.

TREATING PEOPLE AS PEOPLE

We want to create a safe place for unbelievers. We don't drop our doctrinal statement on the front porch of a relationship.

You cannot start with theological dogma and expect people to flock to your side, especially if they believe otherwise. No one is interested in a friendship with someone eager to point out that you're wrong.

In reaction to the past reputation of the church, our generation has swung to the other side. We are friends with unbelievers apart from doctrinal differences. Religious diversity does not bother us. There is an overall comfort in relationships with those far from Christ. I believe this is a step toward sharing Jesus—not a move away from it.

Therefore, we are reevaluating what it means to live in the world. In contrast to being disconnected from the world growing up, we want to be intentionally engaged in our communities.

HONEST TRUTH

One of the most annoying criticisms we receive from the church concerning our generation is with doctrine. Because of our focus on relationships, we are often seen as uninterested in theology. This could not be further from the truth.

The church has misunderstood our generation and the values we hold. For many of us, doctrine is vital to our faith. We are passionate about sharing Christ's love with others. And because of our relational focus, we have many opportunities to share the gospel that were previously unavailable to the church.

As the church often puts their doctrine forward with

boldness, we want to be honest with our beliefs as well. Yet our honesty comes out once a relationship has formed. It is only in the contexts of true friendship that we share what is meaningful to us. We never present our faith as doctrinal propositions but rather focus on the hope and love we've found in Jesus.

From our experience in relationships, true friends have reason to share what is important to them. Strangers who shout religious dogma are a turnoff.

SYSTEMS AND CHARTS

While our relational focus is a huge difference that is often misunderstood in the church, we also have doctrinal struggles in the church. Specifically, we struggle with the clear-cut answers often given by the conservative, evangelical church.

As a generation, we have doubts about and question cliché answers. The church has championed a theology that has answers for every issue and problem. As we've hit adulthood, it's hard to not be skeptical of some of the systems and charts set forth to explain God and His Word. It's too clean for us, too mathematical.

When the church speaks about God simply to place Him on a chart, perfectly parsed out, we avoid it. Our relational focus yearns for a God who connects with us as people. We have little desire to put God under a microscope and dissect every part. Instead, we long to sit back and watch in amazement as He shows us His love and power.

We also know the complexity of this world. There are

hard questions about God and evil that the church should not easily dismiss. Our generation feels the tension here. And we accept it.

Faith that has never doubted is not perfect faith; it is ignorant faith.

TALKING ABOUT JESUS

With the increased exploration of Christian freedom, our generation is spreading the gospel to places previously unreached. Because bars are often a place of social connection for the world, our generation is exploring ways to reach those people. Some have started breweries with the goal of later planting a church through the community that is formed. Other peers are connected to the artist community through painting, tattoos, and design.

Through sharing creative space and exploring new ideas, we are making connections to unbelievers who would never enter the church. These social groups often function similarly to the church, caring for each other with love and sacrifice.

As a general attitude, we are seeking to enter any arena where the gospel is not present. This leads us down many roads that seem controversial or dangerous. But we are not concerned about the stigma attached to ministering to those outside the church. This is the type of ministry Jesus modeled in the Gospels.

Yet the church, broadly speaking, is slow to support this type of outreach. While we agree the church is God's primary instrument for sharing the gospel, often the church is unable or unwilling to enter many areas of society. We carry a fresh passion to commit our lives to meaningful vocation—serving people in a way that is significant. The previous model of working the same job for forty or fifty years is obsolete. Money doesn't mean as much to us. We would rather have relationships and flexibility.

So, evangelism is important to our generation. Yet it looks very different from traditional evangelism. Formal outreach programs from the church will not be our primary method in connecting to unbelievers. Instead, we desire to live life with and befriend those in our community, and show them the love we found in Jesus.

CONFESSION AND LAMENT

A final area of frustration among our generation is the lack of honest wrestling with pain in the church. As a young generation, we are very aware of the brokenness in the world. During these times of struggle, the church has often failed to empathize with our pain.

As I talk with friends and pastors, the need for lament and confession often arises. The church rarely is a safe place for either. As young believers, we've looked elsewhere to help deal with the guilt and pain we've experienced. Often this comes in the form of a social community connected to our vocation or neighborhood. But finding our community outside the church pushes us even further from the church.

The message given by most churches is that they want to help. But the reality is the church rarely creates a safe place for people to honestly deal with life. Sermons are often peppered with examples of seemingly perfect families and spiritual passion. Worship music is biased toward those experiencing joy and happiness in life. The reality of pain and brokenness is uncomfortable for most churches. This is why many of us leave. Our lives no longer match up to the perfection found in the church. So we look elsewhere.

Michael Gungor, a worship leader and artist, recently blogged about this phenomenon in the church:

> When did Christianity become a way of medicating us from pain rather than a way of living within the pain?
>
> Yes, the resurrection of Jesus gives us hope, a future joy for which we are inspired to take up our cross and take another step forward . . . But that is not the same thing as a numbing delusion that all is well with the world because "I'm on my way to Heaven because of the new covenant!"
>
> There is a tension to the Kingdom of Heaven that is here but not yet here. That tension ought to give way to poetry. To lament. To art. Sure, there is room for some celebration, but if our faith has nothing else to it than positive messages and encouraging clichés, perhaps it has become a Band-Aid rather than a surgery.
>
> Worship music doesn't need to be medication. Our worship music ought to put us in touch with the deepest places of our humanity, not simply distract us from our pain and put us in a good mood for the preacher's talk. It ought to stir things deep in us. Hope. Joy. Anger. Mourning. Doubt. Love.

Have you ever had a relationship that never can get past the surface of things? A relationship where the people never talk about anything deeper than the weather or favorite sports team is not a very deep relationship. The people in a relationship that have never had disagreements or conflict are those who have kept their true hearts hidden from one another. A Christianity that does not lament is a shallow Christianity. It is a medicinal, numbing balm that we use to avoid living life in a world that is groaning. It is a Band-Aid to cover our wounds. Fig leaves to be sewn over our humanness. And many of us need to be saved from our addiction to this anemic, shallow substitute for Christianity.[1]

Our generation is desperate for the church to be real. Leaders who share their struggles concerning faith and life. Music that isn't a '90s knockoff, repeating a cheery refrain. We need the ability to confess that we mess up—because we do. We're pretty sure everyone else does too. It just doesn't seem to come up much when we're at church.

Pain and struggle are the common road for humanity. May the church enter into this need with acceptance and love.

Part 2

A Boomer's Perspective on Millennials' Questions

Paul Nyquist

6

Do I Need to Be Part of the Church to Follow Jesus?

Loving Jesus is easy to do. When you read about His earthly ministry in the Gospels, it's impossible not to fall madly in love with Him. He speaks truth boldly and bluntly. He trashes the legalists who controlled the religious establishment. He forges deep, rich relationships with His disciples. He shows abiding compassion for the poor and outcasts. He makes the ultimate sacrifice in dying as a substitute for the sins of mankind. Yes, loving Jesus is easy to do.

The hard question is about His church. Loving the church isn't easy to do. Especially for you as a millennial.

In the first chapter, Carson talked about the many frustrations you have with the church. It seems plastic and artificial. It appears out of touch with real life. It rarely challenges believers to bold action, yet judges those who fail. In short, it's not often a fun place.

You have a more radical version of church in mind. You see this radicalness in Jesus. But you don't see it in the church. You voice your opinions, but your sound is muted. As a younger adult, you are not in a position of authority and influence. The power brokers pretend to listen to you, but nothing changes. As time passes, your hope disappears, swallowed by increasing frustration and alienation.

Finally, you ask this question: "Do I need to be part of the church to follow Jesus? I love Jesus. I don't like the church. I don't really want to exit the church, but I want to remain true to my heart and values. Jesus reflects those values. The church doesn't. So, can I stay connected with Jesus and wave goodbye to the church?"

You are not the first to question the relevance of the church. Some years ago, Bob said this: "The reality of the church as the instrument of God . . . today is met with skepticism and incredulity. Amid the blustering crosscurrents of our time . . . the church has not stood unscathed. That which bears the name of God has suffered confusion with the rest. The resultant widespread weakness and uncertainty has caused many to turn aside, rejecting with castigation the church as the locus of God's activity."[1]

"Bob" is Dr. Robert Saucy. He wrote those words over forty years ago in 1972. While his language is a bit stuffy, his main conclusion would be shared by millennials today. I love Jesus. It's the church I can't stand.

WHY CHURCH?

Yet, deserting the church is different. And that's because the church is fundamentally different from any other organization on this earth.

You likely are involved with a variety of organizations. You may sponsor a child with Compassion International. You may give time to a homeless shelter. You may coach inner-city kids at the YMCA. All of these groups have noble objectives and are worthy of the investment of our lives. But they aren't the church. The church is different. All these other organizations were started by man. The church was birthed by God.

Jesus predicted this new entity when He announced to His disciples, "I will build my church" (Matthew 16:18). It was not yet in existence when He walked the earth. It was not born until the coming of the Holy Spirit at Pentecost (Acts 2:4). Once started, Christ became its head (Colossians 1:18). He lovingly refers to it as His "Bride" (Revelation 19:7). He sacrificed Himself for the church and will one day come to retrieve it from the earth (1 Thessalonians 4:13–18), so we can be with Him forever (John 14:2–3).

No other organization can claim this divine nature. Nor can they point to a glorious future. This belongs to the church alone.

But there's more.

God birthed the church for a specific purpose. It's the institution He commissioned to take the gospel to the whole world (Matthew 28:18–20). In other words, there's a clear task God wants the church to accomplish, and this age will end when it's done (Romans 11:25). To get the job accomplished, Christ has lavished the church with spiritual gifts. He gave some the special ability to be teachers; to others, the ability to be evangelists; still to others, the ability to serve or shepherd. The list of gifts is lengthy. All of these are given to benefit the church. And they are unique to this time. Great saints from the past, such as Abraham or David, were never blessed like we are today. Paul says God "has blessed us in Christ with every spiritual blessing" (Ephesians 1:3). This shows that this age and this institution—the church—is special in God's eyes.

God has powerfully and faithfully built His church around the world. From its primitive start in Jerusalem, it now spans the globe. Jesus' followers exist in virtually every people group today. And it is dramatically non-Caucasian. If God were somehow to allow us to see this global church, we would be overwhelmed. Beside us would be Brazilians, Moroccans, Chinese, Iranians, Shuar, and people from every tribe and tongue. Someday we will see this, when we gather in praise around the throne of the Lamb in heaven (Revelation 7:9–10). What an awesome day that will be! I can't wait to hear worship in over six thousand languages!

All of this is church. A uniquely blessed group of people in a special time. You can't ignore this.

WHAT MAKES A CHURCH?

But I know you still have struggles. You have been hurt by the church and you wonder if there are suitable alternatives. Could something other than the established church be your "church"? Maybe the small group you meet with regularly. Maybe the Bible study you have with a couple coworkers. Maybe the bunch who serve with you at a local nonprofit. Could any of these be your "church"? Did not Christ say when "two or three are gathered in my name, there am I among them" (Matthew 18:20)?

You raise an important question. What is church? In some communities, it can appear there is a church on every corner. They carry different brands. And they all claim to be "church." But, really, what is church? And is it the same as your other alternatives?

In the past, the water was not as muddy. As recently as fifty years ago, there were very few institutions like the church. Parachurch organizations were in their infancy. I am a big fan of such groups. After I was saved in college, I was trained and discipled by a parachurch campus ministry. I owe a sizeable debt to them.

But the contemporary landscape is littered with over one hundred thousand parachurch ministries today. Many clearly overlap with the ministry of a church. They may sound like church. They may feel like church. They may act like church. But are they church? And if so, could they act as your church? Michael Frost asks, "When does a bunch become a church?"[2] That's the right question.

To answer this question, we need to strip away all the external "stuff" of a church and agree on the minimal requirements for being church. If your group meets the minimums, then it's indeed church in God's eyes. If not, then while it may be a helpful ministry, it's not church. So, when does any gathering of believers cross the line from being a Bible study or ministry and officially become "church"?

The temptation is to define church by its form.[3] It's tantalizing to promote a trendy form as the essence of church.

But church is not defined by its form. Church may take any number of forms. A church may meet in a church building or a home or a storefront or a warehouse. It may have paid pastoral staff or volunteer staff. It can be liturgical or spontaneous. It may have choir robes or no music at all. None of that matters because form doesn't define church.

So, when does a group or bunch or gathering become "church"? It is "church" when two things are true.

1. The group formally recognizes it is church.

This may seem like circular reasoning, but it is not. Here's why: Any group can perform some or many of the functions of a church. An evangelistic organization can evangelize. A teaching ministry can teach. A discipling ministry can disciple. A compassion ministry can meet physical needs. Some groups, as they grow and broaden, can do several of these functions simultaneously.

But that doesn't mean they're church. Nor would they likely claim to be church. Instead, a group of believers takes the first step to becoming a church when they come to the realization they are indeed church—when they have a formal recognition, they're a local manifestation of the body of Christ.

This is vital, just as marriage vows are necessary for a married couple. Any two people can live together. They can even do many things married couples do. But that doesn't make them married. They are only married by law and in God's eyes when they formalize their commitment in a marriage ceremony.

In the same way, a group doesn't become church until they realize and agree they *are* church. In so doing, they cross over an imaginary line.

From my experience in leadership with a church planting organization, this realization can be gradual. A group can meet, study the Bible, enjoy rich fellowship, and serve each other for several years without claiming to be a church. However, as they grow and learn together, one day a Spirit-illumined light goes on. They understand they are not just an anonymous group of Christ-followers somewhere. They realize they are indeed a church. They cross the line. Before, they were doing many of the things a church does. Now, they formally recognize they *are* church.

Once this is true, this leads to a second minimum requirement for church.

2. The group intentionally does what the Bible says a church is to do.

Both of these elements are necessary. A group may claim to be "church" and not have any interest in doing what a church is to do. Cultlike groups do this. It's bogus.

Instead, once a group formally recognizes that what they have is church, they must intentionally do what the Bible says a church is to do. They must study God's Word and seek to perform the functions God has given to the church. Initially, the church may not be able to do them all or do them all well due to a lack of maturity. But it should have the desire to model God's design for His church.

WHAT DOES GOD WANT THE CHURCH TO DO?

Deciding this is a real challenge. Good people may disagree with me here. Being a boomer and a former pastor, my natural inclination is to create a lengthy list of necessary functions for a church. So, your list may be different from mine. But in a desire to identify the bare minimums, four functions seem clear for any group who understands they are church.

First, they gather regularly.

This is the biblical pattern, starting from the very birth of the church in the book of Acts. How often does a church need to meet? The early church met weekly, on "the first day of the week" (Acts 20:7), or Sunday. I admit this is just a pattern established by the church and not a prescription from God. However, at the very least it suggests assembly meetings cannot be sporadic or infrequent. They must be regular and intentional. A weekly cycle carries the support of the New Testament.

Second, they appoint qualified leaders.

God's plan for the church includes the spiritual oversight of leaders who meet the specific qualifications set forth in Titus 1 and 1 Timothy 3. There is a list of qualifications for elders and a separate but similar list for deacons. Any group claiming to be church cannot overlook this. They must appoint leaders who meet God's criteria, for they are the ones God entrusts with the care and feeding of His flock.

Third, they observe the ordinances.

We can quibble here. Some call these sacraments. Some disagree on how many ordinances exist. I don't want to get into a food fight here. I like the label of "ordinances" because

I see these as practices Christ ordained for His church. Some may wish to include more, but I see two ordinances in the New Testament. The observance of the Lord's Table and water baptism. This doesn't mean that only the church can practice these things. We have all perhaps been at a camp meeting where Communion was served. But it does mean that a church must observe these ordinances.

Finally, they maintain disciplines that mature and protect the church.

This is where the list could become quite lengthy. But I remain impressed by the snapshot of the first church in Jerusalem provided for us by Luke in Acts 2:42. Check it out for yourself. The church had just been born with the coming of the Holy Spirit and the conversion of three thousand souls (Acts 2:41). The idea of church was brand-new. No one had an operating manual. There was no tradition to follow or avoid. So, what did the early church do? Luke says, "And they devoted themselves to the apostles' teaching and the fellowship, to the breaking of bread and the prayers."

This is Spirit-filled church doing church. Four practices dominated their time together. Teaching, fellowship, the breaking of bread (likely involving both a meal and an observance of the Lord's Table), and prayer. Each practice serves to mature the church while also protecting the church. Teaching equips us but also guards against heresy. Fellowship encourages us but also guards against isolation. Communion inspires us but also guards against forgetfulness. Prayer deepens us but also guards against independence.

I could easily list many other commands given to the

church, including the many "one another" passages. But for the bare minimums, I am content to leave it at this. A group is a church when it formally recognizes it is church and then seeks to do what the Bible says a church is to do. This means it gathers together on a regular basis. This means it appoints qualified leaders. This means it observes the ordinances. And this means it practices disciplines that mature and protect the church.

Now obviously church can be much more than that. In contemporary megachurches, it *is* much more than that. But it can't be less than that and in God's eyes still be "church."

EVALUATE YOUR SITUATION

To sum up, you can't sidestep your need to be part of the church. Robert Saucy put it like this: "The follower of Jesus cannot profess allegiance to Him and deny His Church."[4] The writer of Hebrews agreed when he wrote, "And let us consider how to stir up one another to love and good works, not neglecting to meet together, as is the habit of some, but encouraging one another, and all the more as you see the Day drawing near" (Hebrews 10:24–25).

You need the church. Not a pseudochurch. Not a glorified Bible study. Not a group of friends who hang out together. A real church that recognizes it is the church. A real church that seeks to do what God says a church is to do.

The church also needs you. It needs your passion. It needs your gifts. Paul writes, "To each is given the manifestation of the Spirit" (1 Corinthians 12:7). You have a God-given role to play in the local church.

Does this need to be the established evangelical church? Not necessarily, and I understand your hesitancy. You maybe could see yourself reengaging with the church as long as you would not have to confront the painful realities of your baggage with the evangelical church. An easy route is to find a new millennial start-up church and funnel your energies there.

But let me challenge you to take the bolder course. While rarely easy, you are strategically positioned to be a force for change in the evangelical church. You were brought up in the evangelical church. You were likely saved through the evangelical church. You understand the evangelical church. It is part of your spiritual DNA.

Yet you also have a pulse on the pain and passion of this new generation. You understand the heartbeat of the millennials. Therefore, you can be a much more effective agent for change than I could be as a card-carrying member of the boomer generation. So, how could you help the evangelical church make the necessary changes in order to become a more welcoming place for other millennials like you?

You might say, "I've been there, done that, and it didn't work." I don't doubt that. In the next chapter, we will talk more about the change process, which is always a challenge in any human institution but especially in the church. At this point, I simply want to challenge you to be a force for change in the church. This means you will have to set aside personal desires and adopt a broader perspective. This means you can't simply think about yourself but also how you can help others in their spiritual journeys. This is a Jesus attitude.

The apostle Paul challenges each one of us with this attitude in Philippians 2 when he writes, "Do nothing from selfish ambition or conceit, but in humility count others more significant than yourselves. Let each of you look not only to his own interests, but also to the interests of others. Have this mind among yourselves, which is yours in Christ Jesus" (Philippians 2:3–5).

You claim to be a follower of Jesus. Here is a humble Jesus attitude. You need the church, as flawed as it may be. The church needs you, not only now but also in the future as a leader.

So put the needs of others above yours. Look past your baggage with the evangelical church. Choose to reengage.

7

How Do I Deal with the Current Reputation of the Church?

Every organization has an image. Your image is how you are perceived by outsiders. It's your reputation. It's your street cred. Your image may be accurate. Or it may not be. But it's how people view you.

Some organizations enjoy the advantage of an attractive image. For example, Google is the dream company for many today. It is widely perceived to provide a highly creative work environment while being the cutting-edge industry leader. People line up for a chance to work at Google.

Chick-fil-A has a similar reputation. They take care of their employees and are never open on Sundays. Most fast-food operations are desperate for workers. Not Chick-fil-A. They can be choosy because they are so highly regarded by the public.

But not every organization has the luxury of a stellar image. Or it may be they had a great reputation but lost it. Such is the case with Penn State University. For decades this school was viewed as the model for integrity and trustworthiness. But now this reputation has been deeply stained by the conviction of one of their football coaches for multiple counts of sexual exploitation of a minor. Their image has been sullied. And it will take years to change how they are viewed by others.

Corporate America regularly creates similar issues with its antics. You can pick your poison here. Enron? The banking crisis? British Petroleum? Bernie Madoff? The list never ends.

The problem comes when you choose to identify with an organization that has a negative reputation. Once you wear the badge, you inherit the reputation. Good or bad. Like it or not. Believe me, I know what that is like.

Just after I was named president of an international mission agency, I discovered a sticky situation from over twenty-five years ago. Some of our missionary kids had been sexually abused by one of our missionaries at a boarding school in Africa. It had been pushed under the rug by the field staff and never reported to the home office. Soon after my arrival, it surfaced. Correspondence with a couple of the victims revealed deep hurt, anger, and scars.

I organized a reconciliation weekend facilitated by professional counselors. The first night provided the victims a chance to express themselves to me and other members of our leadership. Believe me, they didn't hold back. Pain harbored for two decades was spewed out like venom that night. They glared at me like I was a terrorist. Tears flowed all evening. I felt I was on trial for the sins of my predecessors, even though I didn't have anything to do with it. But they didn't care. I represented the organization. Therefore, like it or not, this is the reputation I inherited.

That is not fun. You don't want to be stained by the legacy that has been handed to you. But if you choose to identify with the group in question, you have no choice. Its legacy is now your identity.

THE LEGACY OF THE CHURCH

The church has a problem with its reputation in the world. Kinnaman states it clearly when he says, "Christianity has an image problem."[1] While shocking to some, it's time to face the music. Many view the church in a negative light. It's seen as narrow, judgmental, stodgy, and out of touch with the real world.

As a Christian, that problem is now yours. If you identify with the established church, you wear its reputation. But you know it's not too attractive, and even less appealing to your unbelieving friends.

So, what do you do with this? How should you deal with the negative reputation of the church?

In response, let me help you see reality. The church hasn't been perfect, isn't perfect, and will never be perfect. Even when you are in charge in the future.

Often I hear calls to get back to New Testament Christianity. Really? Have you dug into the Epistles recently? It's true the first-century church had some advantages over us. They had the apostles who had rubbed shoulders with Jesus. They weren't laden down with centuries of tradition and inertia. There was freshness to the church experience.

Yet, the writings of the apostle Paul show us there were still serious problems. The churches in Galatia were deeply divided by legalists who had penetrated the ranks. The believers in Colossae embraced heresy. Thessalonian believers were living carelessly because they misunderstood the day of the Lord. And what about Corinth? How would you like to have that church as your home church? Incest. Lawsuits. Abuse of the Lord's Table. Fighting. Pridefully elevating some spiritual gifts over others.

We can't point to the early church as the ideal model. Neither does church history give us perfect churches. A tour through the Middle Ages paints the portrait of a church that truly lost its way. The common man lost access to the Scriptures. The established church hierarchy grew powerful and abusive. Spiritual favors in the form of indulgences were sold like cheap candy, padding the church bank account. It's a dark, forgettable period.

Yet, fast-forward to more modern times. Colonial America is often seen as a fresh start for the church as Bible-believing pilgrims sought religious freedom. But it wasn't free for the African-American. Slavery was a common practice across society, and even defended by church leaders.[2]

You can race through time, trying to find an era in the history of the church that is free from the stain of sin. It can't be found. The church has always been an imperfect product with cracks and crevices. This is because corporate spiritual maturity is a messy business. Individual believers can sometimes mature smoothly (but not usually). But the maturity of a church, with its collection of different believers at varied stages of growth, is usually messy. In fact, it is *always* messy. Therefore, accept the reality. The church today has flaws. Some churches have more flaws than others. But all have flaws. The church is in the process of maturing, but like any maturing person, it often stumbles. It can shine in one area and completely collapse in another. It can show remarkable wisdom in one arena yet appear totally blind in another. This isn't going to change until Jesus returns.

This is the legacy you inherit. Even the ugly parts.

ADMIT THE FLAWS

I know you value authenticity.[3] You want to be authentically engaged with others without pretense or hypocrisy. But, how do you make that mesh with the church's reputation?

Actually, authenticity helps you here. If you were inclined to appear perfect to all, you would be forced to cover up the imperfections of the church with some heavy-duty makeup. Perhaps my generation has been guilty of that.

But just as you want authenticity in your church relationships, you can be real as you represent the church to your friends. By identifying with the evangelical church, you're not necessarily condoning everything it does. You're simply choosing to align yourself with God's institution for this age.

You can be up-front about the truth. The church is populated by people just like you. If you're honest, you know your life is a string of victories and failures. You want others to accept that reality and not reject you for your stumbles.

An authentic portrait of the church is the same thing. It is a growing place, filled with imperfect people who seek to follow Jesus but sometimes fail. As long as we don't pretend the church is anything more than that, reasonable people will accept it. You can do that.

CHURCHES GET STUCK

In chapter 6, I challenged you to bring change to the church. I encouraged you to put the needs of others above yours and help make the church a more welcoming place for millennials like yourself. If you do that, you will find it easier to defend the church.

You laugh. You say, "I tried once to change the church and got shot down. It's not worth trying again."

I hear you. And I'm not surprised you met with resistance. Effecting change is notoriously difficult in any human organization. Especially in the church.

Why is that?

Because churches can get stuck in a time warp and not realize it. Patterns and habits get entrenched and repel efforts to alter them. Deep ruts form. As a result, decades can pass without the church adjusting or changing. Soon they can find themselves touting cassette tapes in an iPod world. Believe me. It happens.

I recently had the opportunity to return to the community in which I had served as a pastoral intern when I was in seminary over thirty years ago. As I drove up to the church, it was like the calendar had flipped back to 1979 again. Nothing had changed, and I mean absolutely *nothing*. The look and feel of the church was exactly as it was when I was there as a young intern. The only change I could notice was the planting of a prominent sign in front of the church, designating it as a state historical site. How appropriate.

Churches get stuck. And if they get unstuck, they possess an amazing ability to get stuck again. Rare is the church that escapes totally from the quicksand.

UNSTICKING THE CHURCH

Change is hard. People do things in a certain way because they think it is the best way. We are intelligent creatures. We learn often by trial and error. We figure out things. Then, after a while, we develop a pattern of how we do things. And we think it is the best way to do them. It can be how we shower in the morning, mow our lawn, or shop for groceries. We have a way of doing things. From our experience, it seems the best way of doing them.

When a group of people agree on how to do things, you develop a culture. Culture dictates how you do what you do. It tends to be self-correcting. If one goes too far ahead, it pulls them back. If one lags too far behind, it drags them forward. But because culture is self-correcting, it has a built-in resistance to change.

It is easy to criticize the culture of others because as sinful human beings we tend to believe our culture is best. We see others act in a certain way and we judge them because we think we know a better way. But, it may not be better. It may just be different.

I saw this regularly on the mission field. Westerners brought not only the gospel to tribal groups, they also often brought their culture. Why? Because we believe our way of doing things is the best way. Therefore everyone, if they are smart, would do it our way. If they don't, we criticize them.

Transfer this to the church today. Two mammoth generations have two vastly different cultures. Based upon their experience and history, both believe their way is the best way to do things. If you are the dominant culture, as is true with the boomers, you often see little reason to change. In their eyes, the culture is correct and doesn't require change.

As a millennial, you disagree. Your experience leads you to different conclusions. But as a younger culture, effecting desired change is more difficult.

THERE IS STILL HOPE

Don't jump off the bridge yet. Change is still possible. Proof of that is the change that has taken place in the church over the past two or three decades. Church is much different than it was in 1985. Since you were likely in the nursery then (if you were even alive), let me quickly list some of the changes that have transpired.

- Worship has been transformed. People used to sing solely from hymnbooks, led by a robed choir. Now words appear on a screen and the people are led by a worship band with an array of guitars and keyboards.
- Church growth has been redefined. A church used to grow in one location before planting a new one. Now, multisite is the trend. One pastoral staff and one elder board can provide oversight to many different campuses.

- Dress has been altered. Suits and dresses used to be the norm. You "dressed up" for church. Today, flip-flops and blue jeans are often seen in the pews.
- Missions has become experiential. The only ones who used to visit the mission field were the occasional pastors sent by their churches. Now, nearly everyone has been on a short-term mission trip.

I could go on. My point is not to evaluate these changes. It is simply to acknowledge them as evidence that significant change is possible in the church. And if you don't think some of the above changes are significant, you did not live through them.

But change can't stagnate. The staggering pace of change in the world requires ongoing change in the church. This is where we need your generation.

Yet keep appropriate banks on your river. The church is God's institution, not man's. Since that is true, certain things cannot change if it is going to remain the church. Our message must endure. Our mission must remain. Our firm commitment to the authority of God's Word cannot change.

But form, style, ministry methods, and even terminology are all negotiable.[4] In order for a church to be relevant to its culture, it must reflect its culture. The current boomer church reflects boomer culture. As boomers continue to age and their culture wanes, the emerging church must reflect millennial culture. This is your charge. But having said that, listen to the advice of John Stonestreet, a speaker and writer for the Colson Center for Christian Worldview: "When challenging old conclusions, assumptions and paradigms of thought, it is sometimes difficult to determine what to keep and what not to keep. We must be more thoughtful than to merely react to what we don't appreciate about the past, or we'll succumb to our own set of cultural blinders even as we despise the cultural blindness of the previous generation. 'We won't do it like them!' is no solution."[5]

Change will not come easy. It never does. Once in place, it can slip away as people default to old patterns. But it can happen, and it can happen through you.

So become a student of how change occurs.[6] Develop a plan. Work it out. And stay at it. Leading change is not for the faint of heart. It takes boldness, determination, thick skin, and a healthy dose of patience. If you can do this, you may never have to be embarrassed about the reputation of the church again. At least until your children grow up.

WHAT ABOUT YOU?

Let me ask you a final question before finishing this chapter. As you work to change the culture and reputation of the church so you can defend it, could you defend the way you are living? If the new church culture was a copy of your lifestyle, would it reflect a more biblical model? Would it please Jesus? Or . . . not?

You have now inherited a legacy in the church that isn't attractive to you. In due time, you will pass on the legacy to your children—the next generation.

What will they think of your reputation?

8

What Is My Responsibility to Those Who Have Hurt Me?

One of my favorite cities in South America is Quito, Ecuador. It is nestled in the Andes Mountains and is one of the highest capitals in the world at over 9,000 feet in elevation. In the distance you can see the majestic peak of Mt Chimborazo, an active volcano. On one of my trips to Quito, I noticed menacing smoke spewing from the top of the mountain. It looked like the volcano was about to erupt. (It didn't.)

Not properly processing hurt turns you into an active volcano. The suppressed pain becomes anger. The anger churns inside you. Your emotions become charred. You develop a raw edge. Eventually, at a time you can't predict, you can't hold it in anymore. Verbal lava is unleashed on the unfortunate souls who happen to be with you. Your unprocessed pain is inflicted upon them. And you may lose a couple of friends.

You've been hurt. You've been wounded by the church. It's real. It's painful. It's like someone has torched your soul.

What do you do about it?

DON'T LOB A GRENADE

Before I seek to walk with you through this, let me remind you of a few things to reset the context.

First, remember this is family. Not your mom and dad, but spiritual family. Those who have hurt you are brothers and sisters in Christ. Therefore, you need to process this because you will be with them in eternity. If you get wounded by physical family in this life, you can perhaps choose to avoid them. Move away. And hope you don't see them again.

That won't work with your spiritual family. You *will* be with them. Like, forever. I know there will be countless multitudes in heaven, so the crowd won't be small. But I also know we all will live in the New Jerusalem and will be together for eternity. So, you can't avoid this. It is best to deal with it now.

Second, remember this is relational, something you highly value (I like that). You chide my boomer generation for allowing doctrine to trump relationships. You are likely the most connected generation in the history of the world.

If so, this is where you can prove it. To ignore this fractured relationship would lead to a permanent disconnect.

Lastly, know this was not intentional. Boomers may have different values from you, but they aren't out to ruin your life. I don't know a boomer believer who intentionally plans to alienate and anger millennials. Most of their offensive actions have been from ignorance. They do not have a good grasp on the cultural divide nor understand why you are frustrated with church.[1]

But they really do love you and would not want to hurt you. This was not intentional.

SO, WHAT SHOULD YOU DO?

It is time to defuse the bomb. Obviously, there are steps boomers can take to mend the relationship. But I am not writing to boomers. I am writing to you, the millennial generation. Here are three courageous steps you need to take.

1. Forgive them.

This may be a struggle for you. It can be a struggle because forgiveness is not natural to man. I agree with Dr. Samuel Storms when he wrote, "Few things cut across the grain of human nature like forgiving others. Breathing is easy. Eating is fun. No one thinks twice about blinking one's eyes. But forgiving others is sheer agony! It grates on our souls like fingernails on a chalkboard. King Louis XII of France spoke for us when he said, 'Nothing smells so sweet as the dead body of your enemy.' "[2]

Forgiveness is not our first inclination. Vengeance is. You have been hurt and your flesh wants to get even. Pass the ammunition, please.

Yet nothing captures the heart of Jesus more than forgiveness. Recall what He said on the cross just before He died: "Father, forgive them, for they know not what they do" (Luke 23:34).

Sound familiar? Like I said before, boomers are generally unaware of what they are doing. Following Jesus means you copy His steps. It means you forgive them.

But let me go further because the New Testament has so much to say about forgiveness. We receive a clear command in Ephesians 4:31–32. Paul writes, "Let all bitterness and wrath and anger and clamor and slander be put away from you, along with all malice. Be kind to one another, tenderhearted, forgiving one another, as God in Christ forgave you."

Paul says, "put away" all the angry feelings you might have inside. The hurt, the pain, the frustration, the judging. Dump it. Get rid of it.

In its place, Paul calls us to demonstrate three positive attitudes. First, he says, "Be kind to one another." Kindness does not throw daggers.

Second, he says, be "tenderhearted." Cold hearts are not soft hearts.

Lastly, he says, "Forgiving each other, just as God in Christ forgave you." This implies reciprocity. You forgive me, and I forgive you. We forgive each other. Yet, even if it is one-sided and others do not ask for forgiveness, we still have an obligation to forgive them. Because God has forgiven us. He didn't wait for us to make the first move, because we couldn't. He forgave you. He forgave me. For everything. The wrong we have already done and the sins we still will commit. He forgave it all.

As those who know the rare air of forgiveness, God says, "Forgive each other." If we don't, we become like the unforgiving servant in one of Christ's parables. You probably have heard this story before. It is recorded in Matthew 18:21–35.

The parable begins when Peter asks a question we have all pondered: "Lord, how often will my brother sin against me, and I forgive him? As many as seven times?" (18:21).

We chuckle when we read that. For we count too, because we get weary of forgiving.

Christ stuns His disciples not only with His answer

but also with a story. A slave is dragged before the king for nonpayment of a huge debt. A debt he could not repay in a hundred lifetimes. He has no means to repay but pleads for mercy. Unexpectedly, the king has compassion on him. The text says he "released him and forgave him the debt" (18:27). The slave suddenly has a new lease on life. Instead of being locked away in a dank prison, as he deserved, he is free. First stop, Starbucks.

But the story takes an odd twist. Soon after, the slave finds a friend who owes him a few bucks. He presses the debtor for the cash. Unable to fork over the money, the friend asks for patience, exactly like the slave had done before the king. We expect the slave to be gracious, don't we? It doesn't happen. He cuffs his friend, tosses him into debtor prison, and returns to his latte.

Word of this gets to the king. His previous compassion dissolves into fierce anger. He bellows, 'You wicked servant! I forgave you all that debt because you pleaded with me. And should not you have had mercy on your fellow servant, as I had mercy on you?" (18:32–33). Moved with anger, he hands him over to be tortured the rest of his life.

Nice story, we think. But Jesus is not finished. He concludes by saying, "So also my heavenly Father will do to every one of you, if you do not forgive your brother from your heart" (18:35).

Ouch. This is serious.

God takes the matter of forgiveness seriously because it cost Him so much to provide us forgiveness. It cost Him His Son. God will not overlook this. He expects this from His children because He has forgiven them.

So, forgive. You have been hurt—some of you very deeply. As a representative of my generation, I apologize for what has happened. Forgive me and all the rest of the boomers. You can't move on until you take this step.

2. Thank them.

Really? Thank them?

Yes. For while mistakes were made, don't be blinded to all of the good accomplished by the evangelical church. Boomers are far from perfect, but one of their strong suits is a drive to achieve. And, by any standards (and by God's grace), they have accomplished much. Since this is my generation, this may sound self-serving. But bear with me.

On a macroscale, much of the growth of the global church has taken place in the last fifty years. Traditional missionary-receiving continents are now missionary-sending continents. This is true of Africa, where the church is exploding. This is true of South America, where the number of believers has grown from 11,000 to over 75 million in just a century. South Korea is now the second largest missionary-sending nation in the world, supplanting Great Britain. If you look at ratios of missionaries per capita, they far surpass even the United States. China is now home to more believers than any other country in the world. In 1949, when the Communist revolution occurred, the Chinese church numbered 2 million. Today, it is 125 million and climbing fast.[3]

Exciting breakthroughs have been seen in the Muslim world. Indigenous churches have been planted in virtually every people group. For the first time since the birth of the church 2,000 years ago, the church is truly global. Who was minding the ship during this jaw-dropping era? The boomers.

As mentioned before, this generation has also witnessed a vast expansion of ministry through the proliferation of parachurch groups. There were over 600,000 501(c)(3) nonprofit organizations in 2009 that were large enough to file forms with the IRS (receipts of more than $25,000). Thousands more exist, mostly mom and pop operations.[4]

The ministry impact of all these groups is enormous. They educate students, evangelize the lost, and mobilize missionaries. They clothe the poor, feed the hungry, and house the homeless. They serve the sick, comfort the comfortless, and protect the orphans. They broadcast the gospel. They build new schools. They lobby for better laws. Only eternity will reveal the sizeable footprint of parachurch ministries.

I know millennials are keen on parachurch ministries. We will undoubtedly see even more in the future. But it was the boomers who paved the way for you.

Boomers have also had a huge role in generating ministry resources for the kingdom. The Bible has been translated into hundreds of new languages in the past fifty years, and millions of Bibles have been printed. Sizeable radio stations now cover most of the globe, penetrating the most unreachable areas with the good news of Christ. Satellite transmissions send video productions around the world. Needed books and courses are now available to equip the global church.

All of this takes cash. Lots of it. The boomers have supplied it. They have given generously to support kingdom work. About 100 billion each year.[5]

I understand it is not a perfect track record. Holes exist in the résumé. But it is not a legacy that is void of noteworthy achievements. Boomers are not looking for thanks from you. But they have learned and accomplished much. As the ones running the next leg of the journey, make an effort to thank them, at least as much as you seek to apologize to the gay community for how the church has treated them.

3. Engage them

You have passion. You have creativity. You have energy and optimism and fresh ideas. You have an expressed need for older mentors in your life because you also need wisdom.

Generally speaking, you will not find that wisdom in another twentysomething. Wisdom is gained through the hard knocks of life. Wisdom is collected through living and learning from both the joys and sorrows. A boomer mentor, with five or six decades of life experience, can provide that wisdom for you.

Solomon understood this. He opens up the book of Proverbs by saying, "To know wisdom and instruction, to understand words of insight, to receive instruction in wise dealing, in righteousness, justice, and equity; to give prudence to the simple, knowledge and discretion to the youth—Let the wise hear and increase in learning, and the one who understands obtain guidance" (Proverbs 1:2–5).

How does wisdom help? It brings perspective. It adds the light of experience and history to any discussion. In short, it can prevent the repeating of mistakes. At the very least, it can make your fresh ideas better. Kinnaman writes, "Often I am surprised at how teenagers and young adults believe they are the first to think of an idea, a cause, or a way of doing something. . . . Eventually most find that their idea was not revolutionary after all; it just *seemed* hip and new. Meaningful relationships with older adults who are following Christ will help to ensure that your fresh ideas build on the incredible work of previous generations"[6] (Kinnaman's italics).

TRAVEL LIGHT

My responsibilities have required considerable travel for me. I have made trips of thousands of miles. I have made short jaunts. I have led large groups around the world. I have traveled solo. I have seen my share of planes, trains, and automobiles.

In all that experience, I have learned one lesson well: always travel light. Carry along what you need, but no more than what you need. The extra baggage will weigh you down. It will wear you out, sap your strength, and reduce your productivity.

That is my counsel to you on this issue: travel light. You have hurt, pain, and frustration from the past. Consider it like baggage. Each pain is like an extra suitcase you are lugging around. In time, it will exact its toll from your life. It is better—far better—to deal with the extra luggage now and seek to travel light.

How?

Forgive the boomers, just as you have been forgiven. Thank them for their valuable contribution to the cause of Christ. Then, engage them. They have wise counsel to share with you. If you just ask.

9

What Freedom Do I Have to Engage Culture and the Unbelieving World?

I remember the day my wife announced, "Carson got a tattoo." I stared at her for a few seconds, dumbfounded. Then I said, "Why in the world would he do that?" I rattled around in my brain all the reasons it didn't make sense to me. The cost. The pain. The regret that leads many to have them removed. At more cost and more pain. Why would Carson do that?

In my generation, the only ones sporting tattoos were sailors, soldiers, and circus performers. Carson fit none of those categories. He was a Bible college graduate and now finishing his seminary degree. He had a ministry heart and a ministry future. Why would he want a tattoo? What was he trying to express by inking part of his body?

I expected Carson would inform me of his new tattoo the next time we talked. But he didn't. I didn't bring it up, partly because I was still struggling with it but also because I wanted him to raise the subject. In the meantime, I learned from others who had seen it that it was on his rib cage and that it was the Greek phrase τέκνον θεοῦ, which means, "Child of God." While I was relieved it was not artwork of a fire-breathing dragon nor obvious to most people, I still wondered why Carson wanted a tattoo.

The long-awaited conversation finally came in a phone call after we had talked about other subjects. It was clear Carson had been hurt by my silence. He said, "Dad, why didn't you ask me about my tattoo?"

And I replied, "Why didn't you tell me about it?"

That broke the ice, and the resulting interchange allowed us the opportunity to discuss the matter. At that moment, I learned something I tended to dismiss too quickly—you as the millennial generation are not just a younger copy of your parents. You are born of a different culture with a unique set of values. You see the world—and Christianity—through different lenses. Seeking to be true to those values, you have not found wide acceptance by baby boomers, such as me. Instead, you have experienced judgment, frustration, alienation, and deep hurt.

HOW FAR DO WE GO?

From my perch, this issue of Christian freedom lies squarely at the core of the differences between millennials and boomers. But it is not as simple as you might think. So let's talk.

Much of the judging you have experienced from us is related to this passion. You authentically want to engage with unbelievers and the culture. You despise a Christianity that is disconnected from the world around us. You abhor "church" that is insulated from unbelievers and operates safely and happily in its own spiritual bubble. That seems as fake to you as a rubber chicken.

You want a gritty Jesus. You want a Savior in the streets. You want a Christianity that touches people where they live and where they hurt. This means you sometimes have to get down and dirty with them. This means you choose to live in their world, in their culture, in their pain.

I applaud this. Most boomers I know (not all) applaud this. While they may appear totally disinterested in penetrating contemporary culture with the gospel, they are not. They get this. They understand you cannot reach people with the message of salvation if you lack connection points with them. They realize God did not call us to be isolated in a "holy huddle." Really. They get this.

The break point has not been in the passion to intersect with unbelievers in a meaningful way. Instead, it has been how to do that in a way consistent with Scripture. Specifically, what limits exist? Are there limits? In our desire to touch a hurting, dazed world, what is out of bounds? Where do we cross the line and abuse our freedom in Christ? Does anything go? How far can and should we go to reach a soul for Jesus?

The path is not clearly marked in Scripture. This is understandable. If rules for cultural engagement were provided in the New Testament, they would be useless to us, for the Roman culture is not our culture. Our questions are different. God knows this.

But this does not mean Scripture is silent here. It speaks. But it instructs us through principles, not rules.

THE EXAMPLE OF PAUL

I wish we could Skype with the apostle Paul in heaven on this question. He was a master at dancing the line between cultural engagement and Christian liberty.

For example, he was epic in his connection with the Athenians in Acts 17. As he waited impatiently for Timothy and Silas to arrive in Athens on his second missionary journey, he alertly observed the vast number of idols enshrined in the city (Acts 17:16). It has been said there were more idols than people in Athens. That may be overstated, but it was a city bulging with idols. Every god in the Greek and Roman pantheon had one.

As Paul strolled the streets of this famous city, he intentionally sought to understand the culture and engage with it. When he was provided the chance to speak to the stuffy philosophers of the city on Mars Hill, he explains he had examined the objects of their idolatrous worship. In other words, he didn't separate himself from these pagan idols. He didn't avoid culture. He intentionally engaged with it.

In so doing, he noticed a strange, nameless idol. It was erected "to the unknown god" (Acts 17:23). Paul then used this touch point to launch into an explanation of the God of the Bible (Acts 17:24–31), concluding with the truth of a resurrected Savior.

Brilliant.

Paul easily flexed as he moved among crowds and cultures because he wanted to be all things to all people so that by all means he might save some (1 Corinthians 9:22). So, when he was with the Romans, he enjoyed a pulled pork sandwich.

When he was with the Jews, he stayed kosher. He adjusted. He adapted. He tweaked his lifestyle based upon his surroundings. You can't be that fluid if you don't understand both liberty and legalism.

WHAT IS LEGALISM?

Often, legalism is identified by a set of rules. Do this. Don't do that. Some run from rules, claiming it is legalism. It is not. Legalism is not the law. There has always been law in the world. Since Moses, there has always been law in the Bible. Even in the New Testament, we have law. As believers, we operate under "the law of Christ" (Galatians 6:2). The commands of the New Testament provide this code for us. And this law is good and beneficial for us, since it comes from God. So, legalism is not the presence of law or moral code.

Legalism is an attitude.[1] Legalism exists when you conform to a rule or code with the motivation of exalting yourself. You may pretend it helps sanctify you. For instance, you could claim a vegan diet accelerates your personal spiritual growth. On the outside, that may seem plausible. But because your motivation is wrong and you have exalted yourself, you actually stunt growth.

So, law does not make you a legalist. But the attitude in which you apply law could very easily give you the badge.

Paul boldly called out legalism when he saw it, even when he had to stand nose to nose with Peter, the larger-than-life leader of the early church. When Peter reverted to a kosher diet in Antioch, even causing others to follow suit, Paul blasted him (Galatians 2:11–14).

WHAT IS LIBERTY?

The essence of liberty is freedom. A prisoner lacks freedom. He is locked in a prison cell and every activity is regulated. Upon the completion of his sentence, he is released and he gains freedom. This is liberty. Liberty is freedom.

For a believer, liberty has more than one facet. In one way, we can talk about our freedom from the power of sin. Before coming to Christ, we were captive to sin (Romans 6:6). We weren't free to choose godly living nor would we have wanted it (Romans 8:6–7). But Christ set us free. Therefore, we now have the liberty to choose a different course for our life—a holy and God-honoring path (Romans 6:7–14).

However, this chapter isn't about that. It's not about how Christ sets us free from the power of sin. Instead, it's about how freedom can be rightly exercised to connect authentically with an unbelieving world. The question again is, are there limits?

THE LIMIT OF LOVE

Unless you are God, freedom isn't without limits. I may be free to live as a citizen of the United States, but I'm not free to live exactly as I please. I can't take an AK-47 to the local McDonald's. I can't steal my neighbor's BMW because I want it. Freedom is never without limits.

The same is true in the Christian life. Paul makes this clear in Galatians 5:13 when he says, "For you were called to freedom, brothers. Only do not use your freedom as an opportunity for the flesh, but through love serve one another."

As believers, our liberty is limited by our love for each other. Love seeks the best for others, just as God demonstrated in His love for us (Romans 5:8). In this case, love limits our liberty in that we choose not to exercise our freedom if we know it could cause another believer to struggle in her spiritual life.

How so? This is where it gets a bit messy. In the first century, a real example was dining on choice rib eyes that had already been offered to pagan gods. Jewish Christians didn't struggle with this, as they didn't come from an idolatrous background. But the Gentile believer? Quite the contrary. Most were steeped in idolatry, and breaking free from the emotional ties to their pagan background was exceedingly difficult. Therefore, it created severe inner conflict for them when they saw other believers eating meat offered to idols. They were "weak" in this area and their conscience was "defiled" (1 Corinthians 8:7).

So, how does Paul instruct us? He says, "Take care that this right of yours does not somehow become a stumbling block to the weak" (1 Corinthians 8:9). In fact, Paul, the champion of Christian liberty, even says, "If food makes my brother stumble, I will never eat meat, lest I make my brother stumble" (1 Corinthians 8:13).

His point: I care deeply for my brothers and sisters in Christ. I love them and am concerned for their walk with Christ. Furthermore, I accept responsibility for how my actions may affect them. I have liberty. But I will not allow my liberty to trip up others. My love for them limits the exercise of my liberty.

The practice of love-limited liberty can be trickier today. The stumbling issues are different and constantly changing. No one struggles with pagan meat today. But what about drinking? What about smoking? Are those battlegrounds for believers today? Absolutely. What does love mean? You have to decide.

I read an interesting story after the Texas Rangers won the American League championship title in 2010. Their all-star outfielder, Josh Hamilton, has a history of drug and alcohol abuse. Now a Christian, he knows he cannot even sniff the stuff or he will be pulled again into its clutches. As you may know, it's traditional for a baseball team to celebrate after clinching the pennant by drinking champagne in the clubhouse. Hamilton's teammates knew this would be disastrous for him. So, in an intentional break from tradition, and perhaps contrary to most of their deep desires, they celebrated in the clubhouse with ginger ale.[2]

I read that and wonder. How is it a bunch of unsaved ballplayers demonstrate more love to a teammate than most Christians do to other believers?

Are you willing to show your love by limiting your liberty? If so, how can you still authentically engage with your culture? This takes more work. But the answer is not either/or. Paul proves that.

QUESTIONS TO ASK

So how do you proceed? As I already said, our liberty isn't governed by rules but principles. As you bump up against a grey area and face either the exercise of your Christian liberty or the limiting of it, ask yourself these six diagnostic questions. I have drawn all of these from 1 Corinthians, as the believers in Corinth had the biggest struggle in this area.

1. Will it be helpful for me? (1 Corinthians 6:12)

Paul writes, "All things are lawful for me, but not all things are helpful."

You are free to do this. But is it profitable? Do you gain something by doing this, or does it cost you? Does it move you forward in your spiritual life, or does it leave you in neutral? All things are lawful. But not everything is helpful. Why waste time and resources in something that is unprofitable?

2. Will it dominate me? (1 Corinthians 6:12)

In the same verse, Paul writes, "All things are lawful for me, but I will not be dominated by anything."

Addictions have always plagued mankind, but they seem to enslave more today. Satan is wily. When we become wise to his old tricks, he invents new ones. He has more enslaving addictions in his arsenal than ever before.

Be careful here. No one intends to become an addict. It all starts innocently. You never expect you will become addicted. But it happens—far too often.

Will this exercise of your Christian freedom dominate you?

3. Will it cause another believer to stumble? (1 Corinthians 8:13)

We already cited this verse. But this creates an interesting dilemma. You place a high value on relationships. You have a passion to engage culture. But should engagement with an unbeliever take precedence over love for another believer? I understand your heart. Make sure you understand God's heart. Weak believers exist everywhere. It takes time to develop maturity. Strong believers have a responsibility to them. Will the exercise of your Christian freedom cause a weak believer to stumble in his faith?

4. Will it build up your neighbor? (1 Corinthians 10:23–24)

Paul repeats his phrase from chapter 6 with a different twist. He writes, "All things are lawful, but not all things are helpful. All things are lawful, but not all things build up. Let no one seek his own good, but the good of his neighbor."

Let's be honest. The exercise of your Christian freedom can be all about your own "good." It is something you want to do. And you know there are no biblical prohibitions against it. So, why not enjoy?

Answer: it's not all about you. You have other believers around you. Will the exercise of your liberty build them up? Will they be edified? Think about that before you make a decision.

5. Will it bring God glory? (1 Corinthians 10:31)

In an oft-quoted verse, Paul writes, "So, whether you eat or drink, or whatever you do, do all to the glory of God."

This means, as much as possible, you want your actions to reflect God's glory to the world around you. Jesus did that. In John 1:14, John says, "And the Word became flesh and dwelt among us, and we have seen his glory, glory as of the only Son from the Father."

You want to be a follower of Jesus. This is what Jesus did. He reflected God's glory in all He did to those who were with

Him. Will that be true here with you? Paul doesn't stutter. He says your eating should be to God's glory. Your drinking should be to God's glory. All that you do should be to God's glory.

6. Will it offend an unbeliever? (1 Corinthians 10:32–33)

In the final verses of chapter 10, Paul says, "Give no offense to Jews or to Greeks or to the church of God, just as I try to please everyone in everything I do, not seeking my own advantage, but that of many, that they may be saved."

If you're seeking to engage the unbelieving world, you want to avoid offending them. Could the exercise of your Christian freedom offend an unbeliever? Possibly. Don't immediately assume they will embrace all you plan to do. Some may be unsaved but still have very conservative values. Would your actions offend them? If so, you've not moved them closer to Christ. You've nudged them further away.

WE WILL GIVE AN ACCOUNT

This may seem like I'm making this too difficult. Questions to ask. Issues to ponder. All over the exercise of Christian freedom. Is this really necessary?

If we weren't accountable to God, I would happily close my mouth. Do what you want and see how it works.

But we *are* accountable. In the same letter to the Corinthians, Paul explained the judgment seat of Christ (1 Corinthians 3:10–15). We will all appear before Him. All our earthly works, both good and bad, will be evaluated by His searching eyes and be put to the test of fire. Actions worthy of Him will remain and be rewarded. Deeds not pleasing to Him will be burned up like tinder in a firebox.

What makes the difference? Motives. Two actions can appear identical to a casual observer. Both might seem "good." But the motives behind the actions could be drastically different. One could be with pure motives, the other selfish. One will be rewarded. The other rejected.

On that day, it'll all be laid bare before His eyes. Nothing will be hidden. All will be revealed.

If you want to truly please Jesus on that day, be wise in how you choose to exercise your freedom. Engage culture, but think twice before tripping up another child of God.

Part 3

What Now?

Paul Nyquist and Carson Nyquist

10

Leaders of the Future Church

Paul Nyquist

Future reality rarely startles you in the way a jack-in-the-box does. Occasionally we find ourselves standing in a pregnant moment, knowing the world has just changed. We had those thoughts when we viewed the fiery images of the Twin Towers on September 11, 2001. In a completely different way, we had those thoughts the first time we held an iPad.

But normally the future doesn't arrive like a storm that overtakes us. It comes slowly, almost imperceptibly, through the silent process of continual change. You wake up one morning to realize the world has fundamentally changed, but you don't know when or how. It is the proverbial frog in the kettle. The water temperature rose without you knowing it.

The warp speed of change today makes future realities impossible to predict. Before globalization accelerated the pace of change, organizations felt comfortable making strategic plans stretching out ten years. Not anymore. Ten days is a long time. Even ten minutes. Fortunately, our sovereign God intimately knows what is ahead. We can only guess.

THE FUTURE OF THE CHURCH

This great unknown is when you will be leading the church. All of us baby boomers will be in glory or a nursing home somewhere. It will be *your* church. It can be the church you want it to be.

But what should the church be like? What *could* the church be like?

I echo what Kinnaman wrote in *You Lost Me*. He says, "The church is called to be the church in the real world."[1]

That means this is not a theoretical exercise. This needs to be practical. This needs to be firmly anchored in the real world. Not a world we would prefer or hope for. A world that *is*.

Megatrends at work in the world today will continue to powerfully shape it, providing rich opportunities for the church of the future. Let me list the trends most obvious to me.

1. An increasing interconnectedness

You grew up in the Internet world. Many of you haven't known a time without the web, laptops, smartphones, and Facebook. You struggle to fathom a planet where you couldn't instantly communicate with anyone, anywhere.

I lived through this transformation, along with my boomer friends. Few understood how much this would change life as we knew it. Excuse us if we lose our breath trying to keep up, but we are not natives to the digital age like you are.

As radical as this change has been, the future will bring more as the emerging world joins the global party and transfer speed increases. The church of the future will need to invest continuously in technology and seize this opportunity to reach more for Christ. And the technology will change. Social media dominates now. But how about in another decade? Not likely. Smartphones are our link to the world now. But will we still carry them in 2020? Probably not. Something smaller, better, and faster will be in their place, and we will laugh at the limitations we had today.

The church of the future will have a street address but worldwide impact. This will be possible because of ever-increasing interconnectedness.

2. A continued rush to the cities

Our world population has topped the 7 billion mark. More people need more places to live and scratch out an existence. They are choosing the cities. Over half of the people alive today live in a city. By the time you are sniffing retirement in 2050, it is estimated that over 70 percent of the world's population will be in the cities.

This means not only more cities but bigger cities. Massive cities. Cities with 20–25 million people in them. Most of these megacities will appear in the third world, where the birthrate remains high. Infrastructure will not be able to rightly handle the burden of the masses. Squalor will be rampant. Social agencies will be hamstrung, trying to meet the escalating needs. It could get very ugly.

Enter the church. The church of the future will need to

powerfully demonstrate God's compassion in these massive urban centers. They will need to care for the whole person, devoting equal resources to both the physical and spiritual arenas. Christians stand alone among religious groups as agents of mercy. The opportunity to expand the kingdom in these cities will be virtually unprecedented.

3. An increasing secularization of society

I speak primarily of Western civilization here. In much of the world, especially Africa and Asia, there is increasing spirituality as the global church spreads. But not in the West. Here the trend toward secular humanism will pick up speed as our society sprints from its Christian roots.

This will create challenges for the church in the future. Privileges enjoyed by the church, such as its tax-exempt status, could be revoked as local, state, and federal governments search for new revenue streams. Hostility to God's people will become more overt. Traditional marriage will be mocked and family lines blurred. Relativism will reign and those who make exclusive claims of salvation through faith alone in Christ alone will be viewed as bigots.

The modern Western church may find itself tracking the experience of the first-century church. That's not all bad, as persecution refines the church. But the church of the future will likely not be coddled or protected by society. It will need to be strong, resilient, courageous, and bold. It may grow smaller at first, as cultural Christians vacate the church. But in time, as was proven again in China, a purified, Spirit-filled church will prove irresistible to humanists who are void of answers.

4. Greater pluralism

The melting pot is no more. When immigrants flooded the shores of America in the late nineteenth century, they sought to identify with their new culture. They wanted to blend in, learn the English language, and be seen as "Americans."

The stampede to the cities today is creating a new social fabric. Gone is the monolithic culture. The desire to assimilate has disappeared. In its place is a rich mosaic of cultures, languages, and ethnicities. A tour through an urban center can confuse a visitor as he moves rapidly from culture to culture in just a short distance.

The church of the future will be intentionally diverse, welcoming people of all colors and languages. Pastoral staff, if they exist, will reflect the various cultures, providing shepherds who know the heart languages. Worship will be rich and profound—perhaps a foretaste of what will be experienced around the throne of God.

I hope that portrait quickens your pulse. As a church you will clearly have unique opportunities in the future. In a way, I envy you.

MY DREAM FOR THE CHURCH

There's still more that the church can and should be in the future. Each generation stands on the shoulders of the previous generation. If you learn from history, and not just critique it, you have a chance to develop an even more effective church under your leadership. As one who knows the current church well, I desire the following things for you and for those who will serve with you in the future church. Dream with me.

1. Move the church from the country club back to the front lines.

This is the current missional movement. God's people have a notorious ability to lose touch with the surrounding world. Much like a well-appointed country club, we can have everything provided for us in church, eliminating any need to interface with secular society. It's comfortable. It's safe. It's even fun as you enjoy the fellowship of other believers.

But if my vision of the future is anywhere accurate, the time is long past for the church to be acting as a country club. Its work is on the front lines, grappling with the harsh realities of a sin-wrecked world. Its task is not to hang back in the refinement of the clubhouse, sipping tea and exchanging banal pleasantries but to stoop, as Jesus did, into the pain and suffering of mankind. Its job is not to pontificate on the blessings enjoyed through faith in Christ but to desperately seek the lost wherever they may be found.

The church was once there. In Acts 2, the believers of the early church shared their possessions with anyone who had need. In Acts 6, the early church ministered to the physical needs of widows, some of the most vulnerable people in that culture. The church was once there.

Move them back. Move them from the country club back to the front lines. You get this. You understand this. We need this.

2. Close the gap on authenticity.

You've labeled my generation as hypocrites. While I may indeed have a log in my own eye, I see it differently. Hypocrisy, at least in its original etymology, speaks of wearing masks— much like the ancient Greek actors did in their dramas. It implies intentionality. It means someone purposefully deceives an observer by pretending to be what she is not. Jesus called out the Pharisees on this one (Matthew 6:5). Every generation certainly has its hypocrites. I am not denying they exist in the church. But I see it more as a lack of vulnerability. Many believers today can appear to have shiny faces in church, while suffering shipwreck within. But I believe the reason they wear the plastic smile is not because they are pretending to be something else, but because they have never learned how to be real with others. They have never learned how to be vulnerable. They have never learned how to be authentic. This is what they know. And this is how they live at home, at work, and in church.

Your generation is different. It knows it is broken and is transparent with its brokenness. That's an advantage, for "transparency simply means admitting what the Bible says about us; we are fallen people who desperately need God in our lives."[2]

An authentic, real, transparent church is not repulsive to the outside world; it is attractive. Unbelievers are fully aware of the wreckage in their lives. They live with the pain everyday but are clueless to a solution. Seeing someone, or even an entire community, who shares that brokenness yet also finds hope in Jesus, is liberating.

For the sake of the kingdom, close the gap. Close the gap on authenticity.

3. Stand firm on the uniqueness of Jesus.

Earlier in this chapter, I talked about how pluralism and secularism will increase in the future. As it does, Jesus will become a more polarizing figure. For a society that preaches tolerance will be intolerant of His claims that He is the only way to heaven. A pluralistic world is an inclusive world. Jesus is radically exclusive. He proclaims, "No one comes to the Father except through me" (John 14:6).

This means you'll be regularly pressured to toe the toleration line—perhaps informally, by embarrassed family and friends or perhaps formally, by bosses, officials, or magistrates. They will strongly suggest you can keep your faith in Jesus—as long as you give up the nonsense of Him being the solo avenue to God.

Resist the muzzle. Christianity rises or falls on the uniqueness of Jesus. Strip that truth away and we bear no contrast to other world religions. A neutered faith has no message.

You have a message. Don't punt it away. When the heat rises from a hostile world, stand firm on the uniqueness of Jesus.

4. Engage culture but don't get immersed in it.

I'm convinced your generation will set new standards for cultural engagement. You'll willingly, powerfully identify with a lost world. You'll bridge the cultural divide, showing dazed, darkened unbelievers the way to salvation. This is your passion.

But please hear my warning: stay out of the muck. Yes, by all means, engage culture. But don't get immersed in it.

What's the difference? How you think. You can engage

culture on a high level and yet retain a biblical worldview. In a sense, the cultural exchange remains external.

However, over time, some seepage can occur. The extra baggage can change hands. Your beliefs are challenged. Then they are questioned. Finally, they are abandoned. And culture has claimed another victim.

This is why Paul wrote in Romans 12:2, "Do not be conformed to this world, but be transformed by the renewal of your mind, that by testing you may discern what is the will of God, what is good and acceptable and perfect."

Believers who are immersed in their culture act, sound, and think no differently than unbelievers because they have been successfully squeezed into the mold. They offer no threat to the world.

That's not what you want. You want to be dangerous.

So engage the culture. Just don't get immersed in it.

5. Affirm the next generation and be prepared for them to make radical changes.

Every generation has good intentions. Every generation follows Jesus in the way that makes the most sense to them. We did that. You are doing that.

Be prepared: your children won't agree with you. Oh, a few might stay at the dance. But most will be seeking to find a church that lives out its faith in a way that makes better sense to them. Their culture and experiences will be different from yours. They'll love Jesus, for He is lovely, righteous, and merciful. But they won't strongly identify with your culture or how you "do church."

At that moment the legacy that has been handed down through two millennia will be adjusted again. Followers of Jesus will trudge forward in a new way. And the Good Shepherd will lead them just as He had led you.

11

Restoring Faith . . . and the Church

Carson Nyquist

Faith will always have its past.

As our generation walks into leadership, we carry what we've experienced, for good or bad. Yet, the good is not always the most valuable. The pain, hurt, and frustration we've experienced in the church can be the inspiration needed for us to create a renewed community of faith. It gives us a clear critique of where the church has gone wrong and motivates us to follow Jesus without the same baggage.

I have incredible hope for our generation. I believe the church is in a unique place, unsure of its place in society as she tries to balance dogmatic tradition and future innovation. In this moment we need leaders in our generation to dream about the future of the church—not to change our faith but to introduce new ways to express it.

Our frustration with the church is not without reason. We've seen false motives, political biases, and self-preserving leadership. Many of the traditions we've grown up with are largely outdated from a progressive culture that continues to change. But there is hope.

The people of the church need our leadership. They need us to lead our generation, especially in this culture. They need our creativity, innovation, and passion. They need new ways to understand their faith, its connection to life, and what that means for our world.

DON'T GET STUCK

I leave you with two things as you finish this book. Each is tied to processing our past experience in the church and looking toward Jesus in the future.

First, don't get stuck. Many of us have been hurt or alienated by the church in some way. We've seen leadership not deserving of our respect or following. The church has left an imprint on the world often associated with judgment, not love. The frustration resulting from these things can be overwhelming. I know, I was and am there.

For the last two years I've processed and processed. I've expressed frustration and anger toward the church. I've questioned whether or not I want to be a part of Christian community if this is the result. I've even pursued other careers—seeking to do anything but work in the church.

In many ways, I've been stuck. I've felt paralyzed on how to move forward or restore my faith in the church.

Yet in an effort to break through the confusion, I've chosen to forgive. Forgive the church for not always representing Jesus. Forgive leaders for holding standards above my head. Forgive the Christian community for avoiding honesty.

True restoration never comes through ignoring the pain or hurt. It only results from acknowledging the truth and choosing to forgive. Process your hurt—doing whatever you need to do to work through it—so you can forgive.

CREATE A FUTURE

Second, choose to create.

Hope is ingrained in our generation. Now it is our chance to create a future. This is the challenge for people in every generation as they process their past and look to what is coming.

We have been hurt, yet we need to get past the self-reflection and lead the church forward in a culture desperate for hope. We need to create. Often it is our tendency to sit back and critique. The church has screwed up some things. We have been hurt. Christianity is not reaching the world like it should.

But our generation cannot continue to only critique. We have to get out there and start making mistakes. Leading will not be perfect. We will hurt others. We will fail at times. We will make mistakes. Sitting back and offering counsel to those on the front lines will mean nothing without taking the initiative to act.

Our faith has been formed through painful experiences and disillusionment with human leaders. Yet, that type of faith is strong. It is based in personal experience and knows the weight of real life. We have a connection to the world and unbelievers that is powerful. And ultimately, we follow God, not men. The stage is set for the church to be healed and cleansed—moving toward a faith renewed with passion for Jesus, not politics.

Let our generation be known as a group of men and women who chose to create as a response to our hurt and pain. Where some have left the church and given up on faith, let us hold on to the truth that human mistakes can never taint the beauty of our God.

I leave you with these words from Theodore Roosevelt:

It is not the critic who counts; not the man who points out how the strong man stumbles, or where the doer of deeds could have done them better. The credit belongs to the man who is actually in the arena, whose face is marred by dust and sweat and blood; who strives valiantly; who errs, who comes short again and again, because there is no effort without error and shortcoming; but who does actually strive to do the deeds; who knows great enthusiasms, the great devotions; who spends himself in a worthy cause; who at the best knows in the end the triumph of high achievement, and who at the worst, if he fails, at least fails while daring greatly, so that his place shall never be with those cold and timid souls who neither know victory nor defeat.[1]

The church needs you.

Process.

Create.

And then follow Jesus as best you can . . . just as those who came before you.

WHAT'S YOUR STORY?

This book is only one contribution to the conversation on the generational gap. We are not the first to share and hopefully not the last. But simply sharing our story without engaging others would be a failure. The dialogue cannot stop here.

So we invite you to join us. To share your story.

Your story matters. Not only to us but also to the church. They need to hear your thoughts, emotions, and dreams. For the church to continue moving forward in the future, we need you. If you want to contribute to this conversation, take some time to answer these questions:

1. WHAT'S YOUR EXPERIENCE?

We've all had a variety of experiences in the church. Whether you're a millennial or boomer, we would love to hear yours. What has been inspiring, frustrating, encouraging, or disillusioning?

2. WHAT'S YOUR DREAM?

Now tell us what you think the church could and should be. In this new culture, with changing values and trends, what do you want to make of the church? Whether you've been a leader for years or remain on the sidelines, the church needs you to step up and create the future.

Share your experience and your dream by submitting them in written form at www.postchurchchristian.com. Hear from others and join together in the conversation.

Notes

Introduction: Welcoming a Post-Church Generation

1. David Kinnaman and Gabe Lyons, *unChristian: What a New Generation Really Thinks about Christianity . . . and Why It Matters* (Grand Rapids: Baker, 2007); David Kinnaman, *You Lost Me: Why Young Christians Are Leaving the Church . . . and Rethinking Faith* (Grand Rapids, MI: Baker, 2011). Other books providing helpful research include Gabe Lyons, *The Next Christians: Seven Ways You Can Live the Gospel and Restore the World* (New York: Doubleday, 2010); Jimmy Long, *The Leadership Jump: Building Partnerships between Existing and Emerging Christian Leaders* (Downers Grove, IL: InterVarsity Press, 2008); Drew Dyck, *Generation Ex-Christian: Why Young Adults Are Leaving the Faith . . . and How to Bring Them Back* (Chicago: Moody, 2010); Christian Smith, Kari Christofferson, Hilary Davidson, and Patricia Snell Herzog, *Lost in Transition: The Dark Side of Emerging Adulthood* (New York: Oxford, 2011).

2. My conversations with others confirm this. Typically, reactions deny either the disappearance of the millennials from the church or a valid reason to do so.

3. Newsmax Media, Inc., "10,000 Boomers to Retire Each Day for 19 Years," December 27, 2010. Accessed August 2012, www.newsmax.com/Newsfront/RetirementCrisis/2010/12/17/id/381191.

1. First Conservative Church of . . .

1. Jon Acuff, "Confessing Safe Sins." *Stuff Christian's Like*, March 4, 2009. Accessed August 2012, www.jonacuff.com/stuffchristianslike/2009/03/502-confessing-safe-sins.

2. Michael Frost, *Exiles: Living Missionally in a Post-Christian Culture* (Grand Rapids: Baker, 2006), 96–97.

3. Anne Lamott, *Bird by Bird: Some Instructions on Writing and Life* (New York: Doubleday, 1995), 50.

4. Matt Chambers, "How a Guy Who Went to Strip Clubs Helped Me Go Back to Church," *Ethoshift*, April 5, 2012, www.ethoshift.wordpress.com/2012/04/05/how-a-guy-who-went-to-strip-clubs-helped-me-go-back-to-church.

5. Charles Lee quoted in Kinnaman, *You Lost Me*, 236.

6. Many of these same emotions can be expressed to describe the

boomers as they launched the parachurch movement.

7. Ken and Deborah Loyd quoted in Kinnaman, *You Lost Me*, 228–29.

2. Christians Don't Do That

1. Kinnaman and Lyons, *unChristian*.

2. While coming at the issue of politics from a different background and reputation, millennials in the African-American community have also expressed a similar distaste for partisan politics.

3. Peter quoted in Kinnaman and Lyons, *unChristian*, 91.

4. Nathan Albert, "I Hugged a Man in His Underwear. And I Am Proud," *It seems to me . . . random ramblings and observations on life*, June 28, 2010. Accessed August 2012, www.naytinalbert. blogspot.com/2010/06/i-hugged-man-in-his-underwear-and-i-am. html#!http://naytinalbert.blogspot.com/2010/06/i-hugged-man-in-his-underwear-and-i-am.html.

5. Timothy Keller, *The Reason for God: Belief in an Age of Skepticism* (New York: Dutton, 2008), 16.

3. Bringing Back Christian America

1. Frost, *Exiles*, 62.

2. Carl Medearis, *Speaking of Jesus: The Art of Non-Evangelism* (Colorado Springs: David C. Cook, 2011), 103.

3. For more information about Kammok and their philosophy on business, go to www.kammok.com.

5. Are You a Supralapsarian?

1. Michael Gungor, "Lamentless Faith," *Gungor Music*, July 5, 2012. Accessed August 2012, www.gungormusic.com/#!/2012/07/lamentless-faith/.

6. Do I Need to Be Part of the Church to Follow Jesus?

1. Robert Saucy, *The Church in God's Program* (Chicago: Moody, 1972), 7.

2. Frost, *Exiles*, 143.

3. Even Frost does this by suggesting a communal form for the church, ibid, 150–54.

4. Saucy, *The Church in God's Program*, 7.

7. How Do I Deal with the Current Reputation of the Church?

1. Kinnaman and Lyons, *unChristian*, 7.

2. Both George Whitefield and Jonathan Edwards owned slaves in colonial America. Whitefield lobbied to legalize slavery in Georgia. See Bryan Loritts, *A Cross-Shaped Gospel: Reconciling Heaven and Earth* (Chicago: Moody, 2011), 17–18.

3. This is documented well by a variety of researchers. Michael Frost states it clearly when he makes the promise that exiles will be authentic. He says, "In an empire of fakery and promises, the followers of Christ will dangerously promise to be a community of authenticity and honesty." Frost, *Exiles*, 82.

4. See Carl Medearis, *Speaking of Jesus: The Art of Non-Evangelism* (Colorado Springs: David C. Cook, 2011). Chapter 9 provides a provocative discussion on Christianese terms. He is right when he indicates certain common words are loaded with nonbiblical meaning. His strong suggestion to avoid such language is one possible solution to the reputation problem. It always creates some measure of confusion, as evidenced in his stories. Other plausible alternatives remain, including filling existing words with new, relevant meaning.

5. John Stonestreet quoted in Kinnaman, *You Lost Me*, 220.

6. Numerous outstanding books exist on the science and art of change in organizations. Three of my favorites are: John P. Kotter, *Leading Change* (Boston: Harvard Business School Press, 1996); John P. Kotter and Dan S. Cohen, *The Heart of Change: Real-Life Stories of How People Change Their Organizations* (Boston: Harvard Business School Press, 2002); and Hans Finzel, *Change Is Like a Slinky: 30 Strategies for Promoting and Surviving Change in Your Organization* (Chicago: Northfield, 2004).

8. What Is My Responsibility to Those Who Have Hurt Me?

1. This is the value of the extensive research completed by David Kinnaman, Gabe Lyons, Michael Frost, and many others. These books seek to describe millennials to baby boomers. Their value cannot be overestimated.

2. Samuel Storms, *To Love Mercy: Becoming a Person of Compassion, Acceptance, and Forgiveness* (Colorado Springs: NavPress, 1991), 153.

3. Much of this I know from my own research. For more world missions statistics and information, see Jason Mandyk, *Operation World* (Colorado Springs: Biblica, 2010).

4. National Council of Nonprofits, "Nonprofits by the Numbers," 2012, www.councilofnonprofits.org/telling-our-story/nonprofits-numbers.

5. Mark Hrywna and Paul Clolery, "2011 Giving Estimated at $298.42B," *The NonProfit Times*, June 19, 2012, www.thenonprofit-times.com/article/detail/2011-giving-estimated-at-298-42b-4693.

6. Kinnaman, *You Lost Me*, 205.

9. What Freedom Do I Have to Engage the Culture and the Unbelieving World?

1. Charles Ryrie, *The Grace of God* (Chicago: Moody, 1975), 76. Ryrie provides a marvelously clear and concise explanation of the difference between law and legalism in chapter 4 of this book.

2. Roger Rubin, "Texas Rangers ALDS victory celebration includes ginger ale for AL MVP candidate Josh Hamilton," *New York Daily News*, October 13, 2010. Accessed August 2012, www.articles.nydailynews.com/2010-10-13/sports/27078056_1_ale-celebration-champagne.

10. Leaders of the Future Church

1. Kinnaman, *You Lost Me*, 33.

2. Kinnaman and Lyons, *unChristian*, 55.

11. Restoring Faith . . . and the Church

1. Theodore Roosevelt, "Citizenship in a Republic" (speech delivered at Sorbonne, Paris, France, April 23, 1910), www.theodore-roosevelt.com/trsorbonnespeech.html.

Acknowledgments

No book gets published without skilled and selfless servants surrounding the authors. This book is no exception. Rookie authors, especially a father and son, create abnormal headaches for any publishing team.

It is for that reason we wish to offer hearty thanks to the Millennial Publishing Team at Moody Publishers led by the maestro, Randall Payleitner. Thank you Bailey, Greg, Natalie, Nathan, and Rachel for your patience, graciousness, and insight. You dramatically improved the book.

We also want to thank Natalie Nyquist who provided wise guidance and a talented editor's pen for the project. You went far beyond the call of duty to help us!

FROM J. PAUL NYQUIST

I am deeply grateful to my wife, Cheryl, who graciously tolerated the demands that this writing project had on our lives. You are amazing!

I want to thank my incredible Executive Team at Moody: Steve Mogck, Junias Venugopal, Greg Thornton, Ken Heulitt, and Elizabeth Brown. You all willingly "minded the shop" when I was consumed with the requirements of this book. I am blessed to work alongside you!

I want to thank my colleagues, the board of trustees at

Moody, for generously providing me the time to accomplish the project.

And finally, I want to thank our great God, who made me an object of His grace and brought me into His church. May this book reflect well on His bride.

FROM CARSON NYQUIST

I want to thank my wife, Maggie. Your critique and questioning only strengthened the ideas in this book. I love you.

Thanks to my dad for starting this journey with me. I've grown to love and understand you more through this process.

Thanks to my DTS professors and peers for many engaging conversations on these topics—Dr. Burns, Josh Howlett, Greg McEvilly, Grant Hickman, and Ty Clark. Each of you has influenced my life in significant ways.

Thanks to Jordan Santos. Your ideas and passion launched this book. I'm waiting for our day to cowrite.

Thanks to Dr. Kreider for the many mornings spent poring over these issues. Your love for our generation is a constant inspiration.

Thanks to Gene Getz and Jack Warren from Chase Oaks Church for your interest in this project. Your encouragement gave me the motivation to pursue this dream.

Thanks to David Kinnaman, Jonathan Merritt, and Matt Chambers for your expert opinions and gracious advice. Your words have powerfully influenced my thinking and growth as a writer.

Thanks to my "Crew" guys—Matt Vohlwinkel, Jake

Hoekstra, and Neal "Cap" Anderson—for awesome dialogue on our road trip to Dallas. I love you guys.

Thanks to Sawyer Nyquist, Karen Nyquist, Katie Kolins, Daniel Kolins, Kelley Duehring, Doug Duehring, Nate Duehring, Anna Duehring, Joey Duehring, and Mona Gresenz for a million title ideas we never ended up using. You were infinitely helpful in narrowing it down.

Thanks to Ben Stewart, Jesse Rhodes, and Madison Alliance Church for their encouragement and support of this project. You are my church and family.

Lastly, I thank my God. Your constant grace amazes me.